The Moon and
the Ghetto

THE FELS LECTURES ON PUBLIC POLICY ANALYSIS

The Limits of Organization / KENNETH J. ARROW
Power and the Structure of Society / JAMES S. COLEMAN
The Moon and the Ghetto / RICHARD R. NELSON

The Moon and

the Ghetto

RICHARD R. NELSON

W · W · NORTON & COMPANY · INC · *NEW YORK*

FIRST EDITION

Library of Congress Cataloging in Publication Data
Nelson, Richard R
     The moon and the ghetto.
     (Fels lectures on public policy analysis)
     Includes bibliographical references and index.
     1. Policy sciences.   2. Social problems.   3. United
States—Social policy.   4. United States—Economic
policy—1971–   I. Title.   II. Series.
H61.N43   1977   300   76–44510
ISBN 0–393–05611–2
ISBN 0–393–09173–2 pbk.

Contents

Acknowledgments

A preliminary version of this essay was presented as the Fels lectures at the University of Pennsylvania in the fall of 1974. I am indebted to Julius Margolis for inviting me to give the lectures, and for the opportunity thus provided to try to pull together various intellectual strands that I have been developing over the past few years. The lectures, and this essay, are based on several papers that were published earlier independently. Chapters 1 through 5 of the essay were, with some minor differences, published earlier as "On the Moon-Ghetto Metaphor: An Appreciation of the Current Malaise of Policy Analysis," *Policy Sciences*, Winter 1975. Chapter 6 has its intellectual roots in an article co-authored with Michael Krashinsky, "Public Control and Economic Organization of Day Care for Young Children," *Public Policy*, Winter 1974. (For a more extended discussion of certain issues, see D. Young and R. R. Nelson, *Public Policy for Day Care of Young Children* [Lexington, Mass.: Lexington Books, 1973].) Chapter 7 draws from an article co-authored with George Eads, "Government Support of Advanced Civilian Technology: Power Reactors and the Supersonic Transport," *Public Policy*, Summer 1971. I have viewed all of these papers as pieces of a larger whole. I hope that I have been able effectively to sketch out this larger design in this essay.

I am indebted to the editors of *Policy Sciences* and *Public Policy* for their permission to republish some material that had been published earlier in their journals, and to my co-authors in these earlier works. I also would like to express my gratitude to

Graham Allison, Harvey Brooks, Lee Friedman, Victor Gold-
berg, Albert Hirschman, Charles Edward Lindblom, Keith
Pavitt, Kenneth Warner, Aaron Wildavsky, Oliver Williamson,
Douglas Yates, and Dennis Young for help on various parts of
this manuscript, and, more deeply, because my own thinking
has been so much influenced by their work. Sidney Winter has
had a subtle but profound influence on the development of all of
the ideas contained in this essay, but in particular, he has been a
co-worker in the attempt to develop evolutionary models of
economic organization, of the sort discussed in the final chapter. My work with him was supported by the National Science
Foundation under Grant GS-35659.

My wife, Katherine, and my daughters, Margo and Laura,
were especially encouraging towards the enterprise. For someone who usually writes dry technical stuff, it was a pleasure to
be working on something that my family was eager to discuss
with me.

The Moon and
the Ghetto

1

THE TASK OF
RATIONAL ANALYSIS

"IF WE CAN land a man on the moon, why can't we solve the problems of the ghetto?" The question stands as a metaphor for a variety of complaints about the uneven performance of the American political economy. In an economy with such vast resources and powerful technologies, why can't we provide medical care at reasonable cost to all who need it, keep the streets, air, and water clean, keep down crime, educate ghetto kids, provide decent and low-cost mass transport, halt the rise in housing and services costs, have reliable television and automobile repair service?

In part the moon-ghetto metaphor is about income distribution but there is much more to it than that. Dirty streets, shoddy repairs, long waiting times and high cost of medical care are high on the complaints agenda of middle-class Americans. In this essay I intend to interpret the metaphor in terms of uneven performance across classes of wants, rather than in terms of uneven income distribution. This essay does not purport to resolve questions. The objective is more modest: to provide a framework within which questions of political economic choice can be considered.

The essay has three main parts. The first (comprising Chapters 2 through 5) focuses on three major intellectual traditions that have tried rationally to analyze problems and provide useful answers. Through examination of these traditions and their interaction with the policy making process I try to illuminate the nature of the weaknesses and see ways to make analysis more fruitful. The second part (Chapters 6 and 7) addresses these problems in concrete terms, focusing on two policy debates: federal subsidy of day care for young children and federal subsidy for the supersonic transport and breeder reactors. Finally, in Chapter 8, an attempt is made to pull together various strands into a relatively coherent approach to a wide range of

policy problems—problems involving a demand for organizational reform which arises out of changing economic circumstances that have strained the capability of prevailing institutional structures.

The first part, in the form of an iconoclastic intellectual
history, takes as a basic premise that the prevailing intellectual
traditions have had less than smashing success in guiding policy
regarding moon-ghetto problems. However, this is as much a
comment about unrealistic expectations as about faulty intellectual machinery. It is important at the outset to avoid inflated
notions about what rational analysis at its best, can accomplish.
In the first place, what is a problem, and what is a solution, are
not questions that rational analysis alone can decide. The questions of what values, and whose values, ultimately are to count
inherently must be answered through political process, not
rational analysis alone. Some groups may be unhappy with their
lot. However, all demands and all groups can never be satisfied.
Some "problems" simply reflect the realities of political power
that cannot be influenced by rational analysis. It is apparent
that the American political economy pays far less attention to
certain values and interests than to others because the voices of
certain groups are determining. The proposal for the space
program had the advantage of not threatening significant interests and of promising something to several. Many of the
proposed solutions to ghetto problems face quite the other way.
For some problems the best we can expect of rational analysis is
that it lay out the topography of political impasse and highlight
the arena of battle.

Second, many of the problems may be intractable, innate in
the particular intransigencies of natural laws or in basic flaws in
human nature, which cannot be offset by any conceivable social
ordering. Nothing can be done about the fact that people differ
in intelligence, energy, social class, color, and that others
notice these differences. It simply may be enormously more
difficult to design policies to equalize educational achievement
or to eliminate prejudices, than to design spacecraft to go to the

moon. For truly intractable problems the most we can expect from rational analysis is understanding which deters us from trying costly remedies that cannot work.

It is tempting to conclude that the power of rational analysis is limited by the room for maneuver between raw political and technological constraints, and that the quality of the analysis can, in principle, be assessed by how well it illuminates that room for maneuver and enables identification of what will work best. But this poses the issue much too passively. Persuasive analysis can urge and maneuver, not merely guide, policy, by pointing to problems and providing interpretations of them. Analysis influences the way the world is seen; it has the power to delude, to misguide, as well as to provide direction toward where we truly want to go.

More than that. A central theme of this essay is that analysis of a problem generally involves some rather strong preconceptions about the nature of problems and solutions, preconceptions that may turn out to be fruitful or unfruitful. The point is not to be taken as a complaint about analysis, nor as an implicit suggestion that analysts wipe clean their minds of preconceptions before they analyze problems. Rather the point is almost the opposite. Powerful analysis requires strong analytic structure. Analytic structure tends to be developed through the long-term efforts of a research community working within, mutually communicating, and further developing, a point of view. However, an intellectual tradition of the sort required to develop a strong analytic structure usually develops an explicit or implicit commitment to a particular point of view. There are a number of different possible points of view, which may be more or less useful for analyzing different problems.

In Chapters 2 through 4 we will be concerned with three roughly distinguishable points of view, and associated intellectual traditions, which see the moon-ghetto problem in different ways. One of the perspective focuses on politics and the policy-making process. In this view, our problems are due to policies that have steered us erratically or in the wrong direction, because they were based on inadequate assessments of benefits, costs, and alternatives. The solution is seen in terms of making more rational the high-level policy-making process. From a second perspective, the focus is on organizational structure. This point of view stresses the fact that the organizations that did the moon work were competent, creative, and well harnessed to the public mandate, whereas those that do the work of the cities are inept, stodgy, and unresponsive to the public interest. The solution is defined in terms of organizational reform, or better modes of public control, in those sectors where performance has been bad. Still another perspective takes its metaphors from science and technology. Somehow, almost miraculously, over the years we have developed technological capabilities to make Buck Rogers real. In other areas our knowledge and abilities seem not much greater than those of a generation ago. The solution is to achieve an effective reallocation of our scientific and technological talent.

Obviously, these are not the only possible perspectives on the problems, but they are prominent ones. Nor are these perspectives mutually exclusive. In many ways they are complementary. Certainly each ought to have, and has had, something to say to policy makers that might grab their attention.

During the 1960s each of these intellectual traditions had a noticeable impact on policy. The search for "the Great Society" entailed highly publicized efforts at turning the policy steering wheel. Broad new mandates were articulated—the war on poverty—and specific policies were designed to deal with various aspects of the problem. The histories of these departures clearly identify the key roles often played by research reports, social science theory, formal analytical procedures.[1] More recent years have seen an increasing flow of proposals for organizational reform: vouchers for schools, health maintenance organizations, greater independence for the post office, a national

---

[1]For a discussion (one among several) of the intellectual roots of the poverty program, see R. A. Levine, *The Poor Ye Need Not Have With You: Lessons From the War on Poverty* (Cambridge, Mass.: M.I.T. Press, 1970).

corporation to run the passenger railroads, pollution fees, revenue sharing. It is easy to trace the intellectual roots of many of these ideas.[2] The technoscience orientation has come later, and never has had the thrust of the others. Nonetheless the intellectual rhetoric has been strong, and has generated at least token efforts to launch the aerospace companies on problems of garbage collection, education, and crime control, and programs with evocative titles like "Research Applied to National Needs."[3]

The last several years have seen a sharp decline in faith, within the scientific community as well as outside, regarding our ability to solve our problems through scientific and rational means. Those who want to get on with solving the problems obviously are upset about the loss of momentum. It is apparent that many of the more optimistic believers in the power of rational analysis overestimated that power. There are strong interests blocking certain kinds of changes. Certain problems are innately intractable or at least very hard. But the proposition here is that a good portion of the reason why rational analysis of social problems hasn't gotten us very far lies in the nature of the analyses that have been done. John Maynard Keynes expressed the faith, and the arrogance, of the social scientist when he said, "The ideas of economists and political philosophers, both when they are right and when they are wrong, are more powerful than is commonly understood. . . . I am sure that the power of vested interests is vastly exaggerated compared with the gradual encroachment of ideas."[4] But surely Abe Lincoln was right when he made his remark about not being able to fool all of the people all of the time.

In the following three chapters I shall examine the three

[2]For example, the "school voucher" proposal is sketched in Chapter 6 of M. Friedman, *Capitalism and Freedom* (Chicago: University of Chicago Press, 1962), but was discussed prior to that and much thereafter.

[3]As an example of the literature calling for redirection of R & D, see *Report of the Committee on the Economic Impact of Defense and Disarmament* Washington, D.C.: U.S. Government Printing Office, 1965).

[4]J. M. Keynes, *The General Theory of Employment, Interest, and Money* (New York: Harcourt, Brace & Co., 1936), p. 283.

broad intellectual frameworks, probing at the elements within them that have limited their power to illuminate, and to persuade.[5] A portion of the discussion will be focused on severe problems within each of the analytic structures that limit their power. But gradually unfolded over the course of this essay will be the thesis that, lack of power aside, rational analysis has been clumsy and myopic.

A framework for rational analysis requires both a normative structure, which helps to illuminate where one wants to go and provides criteria for choosing good routes, and a positive or scientific structure, which provides a map. A powerful normative structure can help in the sorting out, weighing, and education of values, and thus can facilitate agreement among groups even in situations where agreement originally seemed implausible. But delicacy is required to avoid foundering through ignoring or dismissing strongly held and politically legitimate values. Good analysis requires a savvy appreciation of what is at its root a matter of conflict of interest. Otherwise, the coin of rational analysis is likely to be devalued by trying to achieve what cannot be bought by rational coin. All of the traditions under consideration have tended to exaggerate the extent to which problems are technical, and the correct answers a matter of professional judgement and calculation. People whose interests are attacked or ignored by "rational argument" are likely to be increasingly skeptical of the scientific validity of argument that professes to be "rational."

Our ability to solve problems depends of course not only on the criteria for an acceptable solution, but also on our ability to focus on the search for solutions. We need to know not only where we want to go, but whether a particular route will take us there. A framework of analysis serves as a vehicle for collecting and focusing scientific knowledge, but the framework itself is not the knowledge. There has been a disturbing tendency within each of the traditions to make confident claims (implicit

[5]This approach obviously had been motivated by G. Allison's "Conceptual Models and the Cuba Missile Crisis," *American Political Science Review*, Summer 1969.

or explicit) about what would and would not work, claims that are based on very shaky scientific foundations. And when things have not worked out as claimed, public faith in the scientific credentials of the traditions has been eroded.

In addition to their clumsy treatment of value and knowledge (a problem that seems to infect analysts generally), analysts within each of the traditions have had a tendency to combine tunnel vision with intellectual imperialism. Depending on the nature of a particular problem, it may be more or less useful to pose the problem in terms of high-level policy making, or organization, or science and technology. One might think that this would be apparent to members of the traditions associated with these different perspectives, but this does not seem to have been the case. It is possible to phrase these broad perspectives in such a way that they seem to encompass almost all aspects of all problems. Members of the different traditions have had a tendency to be lulled by their imperialistic rhetoric. This has often led them to provide interpretations and prescriptions that the public, and the political apparatus, rightly have scoffed at. Failure to recognize the limitations of one's own perspective has made analysis of problems that require an integration of various perspectives very difficult. Indeed a kind of internecine warfare obtains among the traditions over the turf that lies between them.

2

THE TRADITIONAL
PERSPECTIVE
OF PUBLIC POLICY ANALYSIS

AMONG MANY economists, systems analysts, kindred souls, and a few political scientists, "rational analysis" carries the connotation of laying out alternative courses of action, tracing their consequences in terms of relevant benefits and costs, and identifying the best policy—or at least a "good" one. The utility of such an analysis is seen in terms of providing guidance to policy pakers so that they can choose more intelligently what is to be done.[1] This perspective is closely associated with institutions like RAND and Brookings, the Office of System Analysis at the Department of Defense and a variety of similarly named offices at other government agencies.

The Intellectual Roots

This perspective on problems would seem to have widespread applicability, and indeed those who consider themselves policy analysts seem to profess an almost universal validity for their intellectual tradition. Yet a central theme of this essay is that intellectual traditions tend to involve a greater commitment to particular structures, which may or may not obtain, than their practitioners believe. The normative structure of "rational analysis" rests on the logic-of-choice approach to decision making, drawn from economics, statistical decision theory, and operation research. But the logic of choice depends on prior specification of objectives, or agreement about the nature of relevant benefits and costs. Only after objectives are agreed upon is it possible to pose the problem of choice in a technical or neutral way. The power of the logic also depends on the strength of the underlying scientific understanding of a problem that enables one to trace relationships between means

---

[1] A classic reference is C. Hitch and R. McKean, *The Economics of Defense in a Nuclear Age* (Cambridge: Harvard University Press, 1960).

and ends and to identify salient alternatives. If either of these key elements—agreement regarding objectives, or strong scientific understanding of the topography of the problem—is weak, the logic of choice is not very powerful. A more subtle point is this. Implicit in this basic characterization of problems and solutions is the image of some person or mechanism that is actively involved in steering, in making the policy decisions that guide the ship of state. The image involves both a steersman and a steering wheel well connected to the rudder. In many instances no such steersman cum steering wheel may exist.

The basic perspective is quite well suited to the area where it was first applied with considerable success—examination of public investment decisions in water storage and irrigation projects—although even here some of the latent limitations of the perspective are apparent.[2] A government agency faces the question of whether or not to invest in a project, or the question of which (if any) project to invest in. Viewing the policy problem as an investment or spending decision leads naturally to posing the analysis in terms of cost-benefit, or cost-effectiveness, analogues to asking whether prospective investments of a private company are "profitable" or not. At one level, the mode of analysis involves posing a set of questions that should be explored before making the decision. Thus it seems useful to specify the relevant dimensions of benefits and costs, to lay out the alternative investment projects, and to calculate their worth. Particular proposals (a dam for irrigation) should be screened to see if the benefits they are likely to achieve would be worth the cost, and compared against alternative means of achieving the same objective (piping in water). All this seems both useful and benign.

But at another level, the analytic style involves a commitment to particular kinds of answers and modes of calculation of a

[2]Two of the seminal works are O. Eckstein, *Water Resource Development* (Cambridge: Harvard University Press, 1958), and R. N. McKean, *Efficiency in Government Through Systems Analysis* (New York: John Wiley & Sons, 1958).

particular nature. In water resources project analysis, the position often is taken that while various members of Congress might have strong interests in particular projects, the appropriate criteria by which to judge water resource projects should be derived from economic theory, and the agency head should make decisions according to these criteria.[3] Since the criteria are somewhat subtle, and the formal job of doing the analysis rather difficult, policy analysts are required to do cost-benefit studies to indicate what the decisions should be.

This basic perspective, which sees public policy decisions as "investment" decisions and which also sees the analyst as having a lot to say about appropriate choice criteria, was carried over, with modification, to the newer areas of policy analysis —examination of weapon systems choices, of labor training programs, and so forth. It is fair to say that the "policy as investment" metaphor still is a central characteristic of policy analysis. However, as policy analysts moved into new fields the association of a policy with a particular expenditure has become somewhat looser. The policy questions have been seen, correctly, as going considerably beyond questions of whether to spend, and if so how much and on what. Questions about objectives have become more subtle and complex, as has the mode of analysis. Thus the question of what aircraft the air force should procure cannot be disentangled from questions about the broad shape of national security policy of the United States: what threats must be countered, how forces should be organized, how command and control structures should be set up, and so forth. The investment aspects of these decisions are clearly derivative of the not too obvious answers to questions of purpose, strategy, and organization.

For policy problems such as these, the specification of objectives is a controversial and delicate task. Worse, there is no clear-cut way to distinguish between means and ends. One also can question the power of policy analysts to deliver on their

[3] For a discussion about the relevant benefits and costs, see the references cited in the preceding footnote.

implicit promise to be able to trace with scientific accuracy the consequences (in terms of the relevant benefits and costs) of alternative courses of action. The problems tend to be of the sort that are poorly understood by scientists as laymen. Thus, there is a danger that scientific argument and the opinion of experts may be so much huff and puff, reflecting value judgments much more than real technical knowledge. These problems gradually have become apparent and discouraging to those who originally believed that policy analysis would help significantly.

Attacks on Policy Analysis and the Responses

The mid-1960s were still an era of relative innocence, and marked the heyday of policy analysis. RAND and Systems Analysis were hallowed terms. Program-planning-budgeting had been declared a success at the Department of Defense and was pronounced generally applicable throughout the federal establishment. The progression of three Gaither lectures by practitioners of policy analysis, the first by Charles Hitch, the second by Charles Schultze, the third by Alice Rivlin, traces the decline of intellectual faith.[4]

The logic of choice starts with the specification of ends. The policy analysis tradition has been most comfortable when it could argue that the higher-order values or objectives were set by some legitimate mechanism outside the scope of the analysis, such as Congress, the President, a department chief or the market. As suggested above, the most noted early use of cost-benefit analysis was for evaluation of water management projects. Here it could be more or less plausibly argued that the benefits were more crops or less input to produce crops whose value was registered by the market, a "legitimate" value-setting

[4]C. J. Hitch, *Decision Making for Defense* (Berkeley: University of California Press, 1967), C. L. Schultze, *The Politics and Economics of Public Spending* (Washington, D.C.: Brookings Institution, 1968), A. M. Rivlin, *Systematic Thinking for Social Action* (Washington, D.C.: Brookings Institution, 1971).

mechanism for private goods. In the case of defense, obviously an archtypical public good, it could be argued that the objectives (values to be achieved) were set by the President, his appointed defense policy makers, and Congress—again, a legitimate value-articulation mechanism.

However, the higher-order value-determining processes tend to be ambiguous with respect to precise criteria. Market criteria are relatively precise, but for the most part government policy is not concerned with areas in which it is believed markets work well. Even in the case of irrigation projects, the appeal to the market for valuation information does not fully solve the problem. Economists doing the analysis were rightly concerned that certain of the goods and services involved might be over or under priced by the market: for example, if the kinds of crops produced were subsidized, or the labor that would be employed in crop production would otherwise be unemployed. Further, it was apparent that Congress had distributional considerations, as well as efficiency ones, in mind in writing the basic legislation. For public, or non–market-valued goods and services, the congressional or executive statement of purposes and values generally tends to be vague, unoperational, and subject to a variety of plausible interpretations. Policy analysts thus had to somehow define for themselves the objectives and sub-objectives implied by legislation or by administrative statements. In a number of areas a considerable literature developed within the policy analysis tradition attempting to define the benefits of particular classes of programs (education, health, and recreation are good examples, as well as water resources). In systems analysis of defense problems, clarifying the objectives and identifying what the problems actually were become recognized as the hallmark of good analysis.[5]

While the policy analysts could take the position that they were not really setting values, only clarifying them, or identifying the sub-values implied by higher-order policies, their

[5]See, for example, R. Dorfman, ed., *Measuring the Benefits of Government Expenditures* (Washington, D.C.: Brookings Institution, 1965).

evaluations of projects and policies were not always in accord with those of Congress (or members of Congress), the President, or the departmental secretary. Questions began to be raised regarding whether analysts were not overstepping their legitimate role and interjecting their own values, or specifications of values that were analytically convenient, into the policy-making process. Economists (the dominant practitioners in the early days of policy analysis) were accused of placing undue weight on market data and treating many other values as if they were illegitimate, or of limited importance. Various educational programs were analyzed in terms of the enhanced earning power they were predicted to generate, and medical care in terms of the earnings that would otherwise be lost because of ill health or death. These studies generated sharp, and salient, criticism. A somewhat different complaint was aimed at the bias toward quantification. Policy analysts in general were castigated for biasing analysis of alternatives in dimensions that could be measured, and downplaying considerations that were difficult to quantify.[6]

A more subtle concern also was voiced. It was argued that the very process of policy analysis—in particular the attempt to make the issues explicit and air them openly—was politically non-neutral. The proposition was that the process of arriving at a policy decision involves bargaining, among participants with different real interests, as well as different perceptions of reality. In this bargaining process, questions of value often are argued out as if they were questions of fact. Agreements are arrived at between parties who have significantly different assessments of the consequences of the agreed action. Surreptitious trading is a common property of the process, and a variety of apparently unrelated issues often end up being agreed upon together. While on the surface "irrational," these elements of obfuscation, fog, and log-rolling are, according to

[6]The remarks by Dorfman in the introduction to his volume include an analogy to a description of the flavor of horse and rabbit stew that talks almost exclusively about the contribution of rabbit.

this point of view, socially fruitful and politically legitimate. They play an important role in keeping down fractious debate about values and in enabling decisions to be reached among parties with different ends. These procedures serve both to protect deeply held minority values and to reduce the chance that what is a small cost for one party will block an action that would yield large benefits to others. In this view of the policy making process, the rational light that policy analysis brings to bear on problem solving may be dysfunctional.[7]

Schultze, in his Gaither lectures, acknowledges the political role of the policy analyst, and argues for its legitimacy. He makes the traditional case that analysis has a legitimate role to play in goal shaping in those common situations where the politically determined mandate is genuinely vague and uncertain, requiring sharpening for effective policy design. He also argues that analysis has a legitimate role in supporting certain policy positions and casting doubt on others based on the general public interest in reducing boondoggling, and in aborting policy proposals that are based on faulty analysis or are the short-sighted result of politically expeditious bargains. More sweepingly, he posits that those who take a "rational" view of policy making should have a considerable say in what policy ought to be, a position that goes beyond the proposition that an expert in means-ends relationships can be helpful to a legitimately elected or appointed official in enabling him to clarify his goals and identify paths to them. This position was implicit in the economists' earlier discussions of the role of cost-benefit analysis in water projects, but not really explicit.

But notice that the argument for rational policy analysis now has shifted grounds somewhat, advocating political activism and a revision of the power structure. And indeed many policy analysts have always been of activist political intent, with strong

[7]Perhaps the sharpest complaint aimed specifically against cost-benefit analysis is by A. Wildavsky, in "The Political Economy of Efficiency," *Public Administration Review,* December 1966. However, C. E. Lindblom's skeptical remarks about "optimization" clearly point in this direction. See his *Intelligence of Democracy* (New York: Macmillan Co., 1965).

beliefs as to what the nation *ought* to be doing. This is neither right nor wrong in itself, but it does seem important that we recognize this factor. Policy analysis now is well understood to be a much less neutral, much more active, aspect of the "steering" process than policy analysts originally liked to tell themselves. With the development of this self-understanding, it has been increasingly apparent to members of the profession that it is important to know how policy actually is made, to understand the forces that bear on the process and the parts that cannot be moved, to know where the moveable levers are and how they can be maneuvered. Political scientists, virtually absent in the early ranks of those who were considered part of the policy analysis community, are now playing a growing role. Their original absence is worthy of note here. One would have thought that political science, not economics, would have been the home discipline of policy analysis. The reason it was not was that the normative structure of political science tended to be squishy, while economics possessed a sharply articulated structure for thinking about what policy ought to be. We shall observe this same phenomenon, economics moving into a normative vacuum, in the next chapter when we consider the organizational analysis tradition.

Some political scientists would object to this argument, and trace the modern policy analysis tradition to earlier roots in political science. However, identification of the key policy analysts of the 1950s and 1960s, their disciplinary backgrounds, and the disciplinary literature they cite, indicates rather conclusively the dominance of economists and systems analysts. The new importance of political scientists in the policy analysis tradition is the flowering not of seeds planted long ago by political scientists, but rather of heightened interest of policy analysts in the political process.[8]

[8]For the view that policy analysis has developed from political science, see H. Lasswell, *A Preview of the Policy Sciences* (American Elsevier Publishing Co., 1971). See also Y. Dror, *Public Policy Making Re-examined* (New York: Chandler Publishing Co., 1968). To judge for oneself the roots of policy analysis, see Wildavsky, and "Political Economy of Efficiency," and G. Brewer, *Politicians, Bureaucrats, and the Consultant: A Critique of Urban Problem Solving* (New York: Basic Books, 1973).

Let us turn now more explicitly to the "positive" component of policy analysis. To be persuasive, a perspective on problems must at the least pose problems in a perceptive way and provide criteria for solutions. The persuasiveness of analysis is greatly enhanced if it also claims the ability to predict the performance of various policies in terms of these criteria—and if this claim is not strongly challenged. In the early days of policy analysis there was an implicit confidence that accurate prediction was a hard job but one that could be done by policy analysts. But almost from the beginning policy analysts found themselves in conflict with "experts" in the field they were analyzing —generals regarding military matters, educators regarding educational policy—who disagreed with the analysis. Often the argument was a covert disagreement about values, but in many cases the experts were arguing that the analysts didn't know how the system really worked, and that their models were drastically over simplified. Unfortunately for the policy analysts, their prescriptions, or the programs they recom- mended, often turned out not to work as they predicted. [9]

One response to this embarrassment has been to intensify the emphasis within the policy analysis community on doing serious research on policy problems. By serious research here is meant investigation much more in depth than is possible in the course of a study keyed to a particular real-time policy debate. Another consequence has been the bringing of subject-area experts into the policy analysis community. In the early days there was appreciation of subject-area expertise, but the field expert was viewed as an outsider whose expertise could be tapped by the analysts. Because many of the empirical issues turned out to be complex, and because the subject-area experts resented being regarded as outsiders who had nothing serious to say about policy per se, subject-area experts increas- ingly have trickled into the policy analysis camp—educational psychologists, chemists interested in environmental problems,

[9]Wildavsky reports on some of these complaints. Schultze and Rivlin acknowledge that in many instances the analysts' predictions have indeed been quite off the mark. Concern about this is central in Rivlin's discussion.

and so on. Thus there has been a falling away from the proposition that policy analysis and its claims to efficacy rest on a particular style of normative calculation, and a broadening of the intellectual base of policy analysis.

Concurrently, the scriptures of the policy analysis tradition have been rewritten to shift emphasis from before-the-fact analysis to evaluation of programs ex post, and even to deliberate experimental development of policy. Alice Rivlin traces these developments very well. Under the new experimental philosophy, the role of analysis is to propose the experiments, do the evaluations, and propose the next round. It does seem fair to question, however, whether the new philosophy of experimentalism represents greater sophistication regarding the implications of models of optimization over time under conditions of uncertainty, or disguised acceptance of a strategy of muddling through.

The developments sketched above certainly have introduced a vagueness to the intellectual core of policy analysis. The logic of choice is a clear and powerful articulation of the notion that given a specification of objectives, an optimal decision exists and can be found with appropriate search procedures. Some of the subtle points of the formulation, such as the existence of irreducible uncertainty, or consideration of costs of computation and analysis, do complicate the logic, but even the complex version has a certain coherency. The new perspective involves a fundamental undermining of these notions.

In the early days of systems analysis, when the analyst was confident about both the relevant objectives and the power of his calculus, there was conceptual clarity regarding the role of analysis. As the policy analyst moved into new fields, there developed a somewhat more sophisticated appreciation of analysis—one which stressed its nonmechanical and nondeterministic nature, and implied that what was really involved was exploring the more important objectives and constraints, thinking through the key means-ends relationships, creative uncovering of alternatives, and gradually designing a good policy through an evolving dialogue between policy maker and analyst. The new emphasis on experiment and feedback adds to this picture a dialogue between analyst and the environment. Charles Hitch, anticipating later developments (as he has so often), has suggested that doing systems analysis is a convenient way of organizing a creative search, an effort to invent or discover policies that meet certain requirements and avoid certain problems that themselves become apparent only in the course of doing the analysis.[10] Laying out the decision problem "as if" it were an optimization problem is viewed as a good strategy for arriving at "good" decisions, but the presumption that these decisions are really optimal has been implicitly dropped. However, there surely is a tension between the language of optimization, which is still used to describe what analysis is all about, and the language of compromise and creative problem solving, which implicitly is understood to be the proper language for looking at the real decision process.

The Limits of the "Steersman" Metaphor

The difficulties sketched above, the real ones and the semantic ones, clearly pose severe intellectual challenges to the policy analysis tradition. However, they are not insuperable, and are at least consistent with the structural assumptions of the tradition: that there is a central decision maker who is faced with hard choice problems, and whose decision making can be facilitated by good analysis. The difficulties discussed thus far bear on the questions of what is meant by good analysis, and how to do good analysis. But there is another type of difficulty, of a different order: there are many problems that are not adequately characterized as involving a central steersman controlling a well-working rudder.

In the first place, both as a result of experience of policy

[10]There is an excellent early statement in C. J. Hitch, "An Appreciation of Systems Analysis," *Journal of the Operations Research Society of America*, November 1955.

analysts working in or for government, and of a growing body of research on the policy making process itself, doubts began to be raised about the extent to which government policy decisions could be viewed as the result of the deliberations of a central policy maker and his or her staff. The "bargaining" image of the policy making process, mentioned above, pointed to the fact that there often are a number of people, or key organizations, which must agree on a policy before it can go through. It also became apparent that even within a hierarchical structure with a single nominal peak, if the organization were large and the issue complicated, a considerable amount of decision-making power is delegated, and delegated again. Policies bubble up as actions taken or proposals generated from below, only a few of which can be subjected to top executive scrutiny.

Budget decisions are a good case in point. The view of policy as investment means that policy analysis traditionally has been concerned with the budgetary process. But various recent studies of the budgeting process do not enable one easily to discern the actions of any single central steersman whom the policy analyst can "help."[11] And it has become apparent to policy analysts concerned with budgeting, as it long has been apparent to administrators, that the chief problem of the central administrator is to pick and choose a limited number of places and situations for strategic intervention, rather than seriously trying to "steer the ship" in any detailed way.

Even for those cases where policy is deliberated and decided at a high level, it has become apparent that the steering wheel often is but loosely connected to the rudder. The impact of policies depends in good part on the performance or reaction of people not under the direct control of the policy maker. In the first place, many of the problem activities or sectors are largely operated by private, not public, organizations, and the ways that public policy can influence what goes on are circumscribed and generally blunted. It is not apparent how the

[11]For example, A. Wildavsky, *The Politics of the Budgetary Process* (Boston: Little, Brown & Co., 1964).

government can deal effectively with the rise in housing or service costs, for instance, even assuming the causes were apparent. Governmental credit mechanisms, support of R & D, establishment or disestablishment of requirements or codes, must exert their effect on the behavior of people and organizations not directly under governmental control. In the second place, even for activities generally regarded as in public sector, program effectiveness is determined in good part by the way policies are interpreted and carried out by the organizations that do them. The Secretary of Health, Education and Welfare may make a policy decision, perhaps influenced by HEW's policy analysis office, but what actually happens will depend to a considerable extent on what the Office of Education does, on what various quite autonomous school districts throughout the country do, and even on what individual principals and teachers do. There is nothing that can change this fundamental fact. But even were tight executive control possible, it is apparent that in many cases it would not be desirable, according to the new perspectives of policy analysis. Rather, considerable autonomy is seen as essential to permit the evolutionary development of policies and programs tuned to the special circumstances of the situation that cannot be known at the center.

The new awareness within and without the policy analysis community of the importance of legitimate value-registering processes in determining the direction of policy, the loss of faith in ability to predict on the basis of ex ante calculation what will work and not work, a new belief in pragmatic experimentalism, despair that few problems actually can be solved from the center—all these have greatly eroded the influence of the policy analysis perspective. It is easy to remark cynically that the early policy analysts vastly underestimated the extent to which real progress toward goals they thought were important was blocked by entrenched political power, and by the innate difficulty of achieving certain kinds of goals. And yet, if the arguments presented earlier are accepted, a good deal of the problem may be that the policy analysis tradition was clumsy in its attempts to map paths to hard goals that avoided the political thickets. Clumsiness aside, the tradition was not aware of its own basic perceptions and the limits they imposed. The perceptions of policy analysis now are much more eclectic, and more subtle, than they used to be. No one really believes any more that most of our problems could be solved if only a good systems analyst had the czar's (or the president's) ear. But the newly evolving perceptual frame is less sharp than the old one, and blurs imperceptibly into the two traditions we shall discuss next.

3

THE ORGANIZATION
AND CONTROL
OF ECONOMIC ACTIVITY

Wʜɪʟᴇ ᴛʜᴇ original policy analysis perspective sees high-level decision makers as the key to what is going on, and takes particular policies as the variables for manipulation, the organizational perspective downplays the role of any single decision-making body and treats decisions, and the way they are carried out, as largely endogenous, predetermined by basic institutional structure. The performance of any economic sector is seen as determined largely by two conceptually separable pieces of institutional apparatus.[1] One of these is the machinery for determining demand—for evaluating what is worth what cost and what is better than what, and for monitoring resource flows into the sector. The other is the supply machinery that is responsible for providing what is demanded, or determining what is offered. These pieces of apparatus are seen as built into the sector at a rather basic level. Given organizational structure, public policy can try to achieve its aims by imposing various demands on the system through the demand apparatus. Or it can try to influence parameters that determine the nature of the supply adjustment. However, in the problem cases we are concerned with here, it apparently has proved difficult to obtain desired results by pushing or pulling on the existing institutional machinery. The problem, viewed this way, thus calls for overhaul or replacement of that machinery or parts of it, that is, for "organizational" change.

The Organizational Perspective

It is apparent in retrospect that the policy analysis movement was itself a proposal for "reorganization" in the public sector. The proposal was not merely that a particular kind of

[1]This characterization fits most immediately the economists' concept of an economic system, or the organization of an industry. Other intellectual structures that take roughly this form will be discussed later in this section.

study be made regarding a particular decision. The proposal was for the establishment of policy analysis offices in government agencies to take continuing responsibility for doing these studies, and for linking these with decision making through a program-planning-budgeting system. Several of the criticisms of the policy analysis perspective examined in the preceding chapter were objections to this organizational proposal.

Increasingly, the policy analysis community has been taking an organizational perspective on the problems it analyzes. The questions posed have changed: from "Is this education program a good idea?" to "Are educational vouchers to give more weight to parental judgment a good idea, and what other changes in the structure of the traditional public education system would be necessary in order to make increased consumer choice effective in drawing forth responses from the system?"; from "Should the government spend x million dollars on medical education?" to "How can we get patients and doctors to consider costs more seriously in making medical decisions?"

However, note that in changing the perspective we change the whole mode of analysis as well. While the "logic of choice" description of the task of analysis can be preserved as more or less a tautology, the core of analysis of alternatives becomes the prediction of how alternative organizational structures will behave over a not inconsiderable period of time. Engineering or operations research calculations play a minimal role in this kind of analysis; prediction of human and organizational behavior under different regimes becomes the heart of the matter. And given the diverse and long-run nature of organizational output and input, the criteria for choice among alternatives obviously also are much more complex than those involved in analysis of well defined and limited "projects" or "programs."[2]

[2]In the field of economics, this distinction between choice of a particular policy and choice of a way of making policy decisions is stressed in J. Buchanan and G. Tullock, *The Calculus of Consent* (Ann Arbor: University of Michigan Press, 1962).

Why the Economists' Arguments Carry So Much Weight

A variety of intellectual traditions have tried to come to grips with aspects of the problem of organizational choice. In contrast to policy analysis, where it is possible to identify one dominant root tradition that has been augmented by a number of more diverse sources, there are traditions of organizational analysis in sociology, political science, and economics, all of which have developed independently. Often, practitioners in different disciplines have been oblivious of each other's existence. A scan of the list of recent organizational reform proposals that have been taken seriously indicates that, of these, the economics-based tradition has been by far the most influential. It is interesting to explore why.

Perhaps a sufficient reason for the lack of influence of the sociological tradition has been that on the one hand it is normatively weak, while on the other hand, it lacks a theoretical structure for generating predicitions of the consequences of organizational changes, in the dimensions of most interest to policy makers. Much of what normative structure does exist is basically conservative, treating the existence and survival of what is as an indicator of its value to the larger system.[3] The sociologists studying, for example, medicine, have tended to bend over backwards to describe and theorize about what is, and why it is that way, and to avoid comments on what should be, or even serious predictions as to the consequences of well-specified (but presently nonexistent) changes in the structure. (It is interesting that this philosophy of avoiding normative commentary, and eschewing consideration of hypothetical alternatives, while traditional in most contemporary American sociology, has not carried over to sociological work concerned

[3]For a selective survey of some of the sociological literature on organization and the relationship between organization and the larger social system, see A. Stinchcombe, "Social Structure and Organizations," in J. March, ed., *Handbook of Organizations* (Chicago: Rand McNally, 1965).

with business organization and done largely in business schools.)[4] As a result, despite the fact that many sociologists have strong feelings about what should be done and feel that their "science" is important to questions of policy, the nature of sociology's analytic structure has ceded the terrain to others.

The situation in political science is more complicated. From the perspective of this essay, basic questions about political economic choice can be posed quite fruitfully in terms of how to improve the governance of particular sectors or activities. Until recently, however, political scientists have not structured their analysis of demand-articulation, policy-making processes in this way, but rather in terms of the working of various levels and parts of political apparatus (like local government, or the presidency) that oversee a complex mix of sectors and activities. The studies of supply organization, or of public administration, do fit many of the problems discussed here. Indeed, the normative language of the public administration studies should have a familiar ring to policy analysts. The desideratum of good administration has been seen as the effective carrying out of policies set by the President (or Governor) and Congress (or by the legitimate democratic political machinery more generally).[5] Herbert Simon, writing almost thirty years ago, argued that the key tasks of administration are to clarify and set intermediate goals, examine alternative ways of achieving them, and choose "rationally."[6] In effect, the public administration tradition staked out much the same ground as the early policy analysis tradition.

However, at least as far back as Woodrow Wilson's scholarly

---

[4]See, for example, H. J. Leavitt, "Applied Organizational Change in Industry: Structural, Technological, and Organizational Approaches," in J. March, *Handbook of Organizations*.

[5]For a sketch of recent developments, see H. A. Simon, "The Changing Theory and the Changing Practice of Public Administration," in I. Pool, ed., *Contemporary Political Science* (New York: McGraw-Hill Book Co., 1967). The development of pluralistic theories of governance—for example, R. Dahl, *Who Governs* (New Haven: Yale University Press, 1961)—holds the promise of bringing together these two sides of political science.

[6]H. A. Simon, *Administrative Behavior* (New York: Macmillan Co., 1945).

forays, the semi-independence of the "administrative" apparatus was recognized, and increasingly the delicate problem of the legitimate scope of the "professional" or "expert" became a major concern within the public administration tradition. As a result, the administrative science tradition was as vulnerable as the policy analysis tradition to the growing worries about how goals are set and the nature of legitimate political decision-making process.

Concern that the political apparatus is generating pernicious or ill-conceived demands poses a real dilemma. On the one hand, one can take the policies as legitimate, even if ill conceived and inequitable. But on the other hand, once the significant innate range of independent judgment and action of an administrative agency is recognized, it surely is worrisome to pose the objective of good administration in terms of efficient responsiveness to the demands of that political apparatus. Once one recognizes that the administrative structure is itself a major influence on the thinking of the political apparatus, the issue becomes even more complicated. Administrative agencies are themselves political actors. Traditional American political science's understanding of the meaning of "good policy" cannot resolve the dilemma. From the beginning the political problem has been posed in terms of how to reconcile conflicting interests—hence the concentration on legitimate process. Notions of a "public interest" occasionally have sneaked in, but much of the recent work within political science on this question has been concerned with knocking down simple-minded concepts of "a public interest," and reaffirming the proposition that policy decisions essentially involve who is going to gain and who is going to lose.

The belief that decisions involve conflict of interest and that choice of any form of decision-making machinery essentially involves a division of power is partially right. However, it makes virtually impossible any "rational" discussion of demand machinery. Economists, who in certain of their bodies of literature are in full sympathy with this position (indeed, much of the

intellectual equipment used by political scientists to under-
mine the concept of the public interest has been borrowed from
Kenneth Arrow), also, however, have some notions about efficiency of demand-generating machinery.[7] And by stressing
their "efficiency" arguments, economists have been able to take
over the discussion of how decisions should be made, as described in the section on policy analysis. The consequence has
been a partial cooptation of the normative structure of public
administration.

The cooptation is by no means complete. The kinds of
arguments against the usurpation of power by policy analysts
considered in the preceding section have come in good part
from political scientists. But a sophisticated cynicism is no
substitute for a powerful normative-structure.

At the same time that the grip on criteria was loosening and
the issue largely being handed over to the economist–policy
analyst, the public administration tradition became increasingly aware that the range of organizational supply alternatives
was vastly greater than it originally and implicitly had assumed.
That tradition also has been overawed by the problems of
understanding how these different alternatives might work out.
In the early days of public administration, it implicitly was
assumed that public programs ought to be, and were, run by
public agencies. The search was for an efficient bureaucratic
structure. Even in those days there should have been apparent
the seeds of the complex system of mixed federal-state,
public-private organization that later came to dominate many
areas. Such a mixed system existed then, for example, in agriculture and in higher education. But the tendency to define
the field in terms of public administration naturally led to a
narrowing of vision. Even with respect to prediction of consequences and evaluation of alternative bureaucratic arrangements, the theoretical structure of public administration was
suspect. Faced with the new diversity, the scholar of public

[7] K. J. Arrow, *Social Choice and Individual Values* (New York: John Wiley
and Sons, 1951).

administration, like the sociologist, fell back on description. Thus there are splendid accounts of how federal agencies, like those of the armed forces, increasingly have been contracting for work through private companies. There are good discussions of the increasingly complicated network of decision making and fund flow among the various levels of government and the various private grant-receiving groups (like scientists). But there is no persuasive analysis of how the system would in fact have worked had it otherwise evolved.[8]

Thus, while it has the form of a discipline that purports to be helpful regarding the guidance of policy, public administration has lacked two essential components of an effective intellectual structure—a useful normative apparatus, and an ability to make persuasive predictions.

More or less by default the field has been left free for intellectual takeover by economists whose focus, theoretical and empirical, has been on economic sectors when demand is organized through choice of individual consummer and supply through free enterprise. The unit of analysis—the industry or sector—tends to be of the right size for the policy problems under consideration. Economics has a well-worked-out system of criteria for choice. And there is a powerful theoretical structure purporting to predict how a market-organized sector works, which, given the criteria, provides a complete argument in favor of it versus (an unspecified set of) other alternatives. Faced with thorny problems of how to make judgments about programs that affect different people in different ways, there is much appeal to policy makers in the proposal for demand generation: let the people who will be most affected themselves decide what should be procurred. Thus, vouchers in education and fiscal federalism. With growing publicity about the difficulties controlling large cumbersome governmental organizations, the idea of relying on free enterprise supply, guided by the

[8]Two classic studies in this tradition, neither of which comes to grips with alternatives, are: H. A. Kaufman, *The Forest Ranger* (Baltimore: John Hopkins University Press, 1960), and M. Myerson and E. Banfield, *Politics, Planning and the Public Interest* (New York: Collier Macmillan, 1951).

profit incentive and appropriate prices, is very attractive. Thus, proposals that government agencies use more private contractors, establish health maintenance organizations, deregulate transport, relax housing codes, and establish pollution charges rather than antipollution regulations.

The economists' argument for the efficacy of market-guided supply and consumer sovereignty over demand is sophisticated and persuasive, both theoretically and empirically, for activities and sectors that meet certain conditions. The theoretical literature usually has taken considerable care to spell out what those conditions are.[9] However, this literature tends to state the premises quite formally, and seldom explores their empirical and institutional meaning any depth. Perhaps because most empirical research in economics has been concerned with sectors so organized, and perhaps in part because of a quite natural tendency to see one's intellectual field of study as critical, economists have had a tendency to exaggerate the share of the economy that is actually organized like the market model, and often to argue, without detailed study of the conditions, that those sectors that are not market organized ought to be.[10] The latter point has a certain slipperiness. On the one hand, it is recognized that in many sectors the conditions necessary for the good working of a market system may not hold automatically; there are a variety of possibilities for "market failure." On the other hand, the economist comes equipped with a variety of patent medicines for dealing with market-failure problems within the basic framework of a sector organized by markets: antitrust for monopoly, taxes and subsidies for externalities, and so on. It must be recognized, however, that the great efficacy alleged for marketlike organization rests on two empirical propositions. One is that the market-failure

[9] See for example, K. J. Arrow's statement, "The Organization of Economic Activity: Issue Pertinent to the Choice of Market Versus NonMarket Allocation," in R. Havemann and J. Margolis, eds., *Public Expenditures and Policy Analysis* (Chicago: Markham Publishing Co., 1970).

[10] The most striking example is, of course, Martin Friedman. See his *Capitalism and Freedom* (Chicago: University of Chicago Press, 1962).

problems are not very serious in most sectors; second, that the remedies for these problems often are easy to apply and effective.

Oversell of a Narrow Perspective

If political scientists can be accused of seeing the hand of formal government everywhere, and the need for it almost everywhere, the economist can be accused of arguing away the need for government almost anywhere, and advocating the almost universal superiority of the hidden hands of consumer sovereignty and competition among suppliers to meet consumer demands. There are, of course, questions about income distribution. These, however, are not fundamental. It certainly is possible at least in principle to combine the economist's organizational proposal with an equitable income-redistribution scheme. The real problems reside in the basic limitations of the organizational form itself.

In the first place, where the good or service in question is not strictly private, in the sense that it is divisible and the benefits and costs of the acquisition or use of any unit fall largely on one compact decision-making group, demand decisions made by individual consumers acting independently cannot adequately register the net benefits. Economists of course would concede that "public" goods require collective demand decisions. The question is the range of goods that have such strong public properties as to require "public" machinery. Economists (and political scientists) have argued quite persuasively that the provision of "local" public goods and externalities often can be worked out by voluntary agreement among parties, and that for many goods and services where demand articulation presently involves a collective decision-making apparatus, only a small subset of that collective group is strongly interested in the product or service.[11] However, many of the

[11]For an analysis along these lines, see J. Buchanan and G. Tullock, *The Calculus of Consent* (Ann Arbor: University of Michigan Press, 1962).

problem sectors are just those for which these propositions do not apply; in these sectors, there is no single person, or small compact group of persons, who receives and pays the lion's share of the benefits and costs, and hence should be in a position to judge what is worth the cost. The pollution problem, for example, stems from decisions to buy (or produce) by individuals or small groups who bear a trivial share of the pollution costs they generate; the affected group is large and diverse. The benefits of mass transport go to those who ride, to those who experience less congestion because others ride, and to those who value the option of riding should they need to. An appeal to "consumer sovereignty" and to possibilities for voluntary mutually beneficial arrangements does not solve the problem of how these diverse interests are in fact to be counted and made effective.

Economists tend to respond by proposing that private demand be augmented by a pollution or congestion tax. But they are mute about the organizational apparatus that is to set that tax. To deal with that question explicitly is to expose the real issues under the surface simplicity of the proposal.

There is also a problem at another level. The conventional wisdom is that no one knows self-interest better than the person or group affected, but there are serious reasons to doubt that this holds in all cases. In medicine, patients delegate much decision-making authority to doctors. Many parents know little about what goes on in the school their children are attending, and have little information and knowledge on which to judge alternatives; clearly, parental choice cannot bear the full weight of the decision mechanism. Indeed, in a large number of our problem sectors there is reason to doubt that consumers or voters have enough knowledge to make good choices. While there are reasons to be wary of delegating decisions to "professionals" or to elected officials, the question of how to get good information from professionals, or how to organize governments that are not self-serving, is a difficult one that cannot be solved by a simple appeal to consumer sovereignty. It is rather surprising that economists, who are such staunch advocates of the professional's role in policy making (their own role), should forget their own arguments so easily.

Nor does reliance on for-profit enterprise seem a general solution to the problem of supply organization. The case for for-profit supply is strong where the good or service in question is easily evaluated by consumers, and where there is considerable competition among suppliers. Where these conditions do not hold, there is good reason to adopt regimes of supply organization that can internalize, to some extent, the demanders' interests—governmental or not-for-profit forms, or other mechanisms of public control that damp or channel the profit motive. It is interesting that private medicine is accepted largely because people (in their role as patients) do not believe that doctors are trying to maximize profit but rather are motivated and are disciplined by their profession, to work in the patient's interest. Most private schools would appear to be not for profit, or at least to profess that their objective is education, not money for the school owner. In public-service areas such as urban mass transport where there is a tendency toward natural monopoly, unregulated private enterprise has proved politically unacceptable as a mode of supply, and probably with good reason.

In those sectors and activities where we have adopted consumer purchase plus private organization of supply, we increasingly have supplemented or constrained consumer choice or profit incentives with various modes of governmental regulation. Our actual market sectors are much less like the textbook models than many economists seem to believe. While we now are more aware than before of the inefficiencies of regulation, and in some cases its downright perniciousness in terms of the public interest, it is hard to see that it is easily dispensed with in all cases or that the proposed alternatives really will solve the problems. While there are serious doubts about the way we have gone about regulating the influx of new pharmaceuticals, pesticides, and so forth, new medical technologies and environmental concerns certainly preclude abandoning all forms of regulation of substances that may be very dangerous. There is appeal in the idea of not regulating details from the center so much, and in effect making a better market for the benefits and costs that concern the regulators. But such a "market" still requires that someone make it. A pollution tax scheme will require a regulatory agency to set rates (within broad limits established by political bodies) and to monitor the system. And a "political" decision is needed to set the broad criteria for the "market."

Finally, the implicit argument that the problems are concentrated in nonmarket sectors is empirically false. Many of the current problems reside in sectors where we presently have a market organization on the demand and supply side, and this mode of organization does not seem to be working well. It is hard to believe that the problems with housing costs have arisen simply because of governmental interference in a private enterprise sector that otherwise would be performing splendidly. The television and automobile repair problem relates to activities organized privately. The pollution problem is in good part the result of private-sector activities. This is not to say that the problem could easily be cured by socializing economic activity. But neither are the present problems with our nonmarket sectors to be resolved by making all of them private enterprises. Indeed it is not quite clear what the terms here really mean. Government agencies procure from and contract with private firms, which in turn are regulated in many ways, and which benefit from a variety of public or government-subsidized activities.

The Current Malaise in Analysis of Organizational Structure

It is increasingly apparent that we lack even a language that will enable us to list, and talk about, organizational alternatives in a helpful manner. At the higher administrative levels it does seem meaningful to think about demand (value-determining, resource-flow-monitoring) machinery, and supply (goods-providing, program-effecting) machinery. However, in some sectors it is difficult to keep even these broadly defined lines distinguished. For example, is a governmental department secretary part of the policy-setting, or the administrative, apparatus? How does one treat the dual role of a doctor in determining what treatment is to be provided, and in providing it, in assessing what is in the patient's best interest, and in earning his or her own income from the fees? But these difficulties are small compared with the gross inadequacy of traditional categories for describing organization of demand and supply. Private demand versus collective demand, production for profit versus governmental supply—these categories do not adequately characterize the meaningful choices. To regulate or not to regulate is a silly question. We must learn to develop a richer and more useful categorization of organizational alternatives.[12]

And there is a formidable research task involved in learning to predict, even to very rough accuracy, how different organizational regimes will perform under different circumstances. As suggested earlier, a good part of the appeal of the economists' organizational proposal is that it purports to rest on a reliable predictive framework. There are powerful reasons to doubt that the economists' predictive model is anywhere near as good as advertised. When pressed even economists become modest nowadays, and admit that they have confidence in their predictive theory only in sectors where conditions approximate perfect competition (and there are reasons for some doubts even there). Most market-organized sectors do not evolve such a structure, and under conditions of oligopoly or monopoly a wide range of behavior patterns is possible. But the merits of market organization, and the problems that must be dealt with

[12]One striking exception to the rule that social scientists have tended to view organizational choices as limited is R. Dahl and C. E. Lindblom, *Politics, Economics and Welfare* (New York: Harper & Row, 1953). A. O. Hirschman's terms "exit" and "voice" may be part of a richer vocabulary needed for characterization. See his *Exit, Voice, and Loyalty* (Cambridge: Harvard University Press, 1970).

by ancillary structures like regulation, are highly sensitive to the way firms behave. Various theories of behavior imply quite different "anatomies of market failure."

The question of prediction, and the question of appropriate criteria for choice, are of course not independent. A useful normative framework must be affiliated with a scientific structure that can predict the consequences of various alternatives in the dimensions relevant to the criteria for choice. The organizational analysis tradition has an especially hard predictive requirement, since it must predict performance of different organizational regimes over a relatively long time. A key commitment of the organizational viewpoint is that major changes in the basic organization of a sector are not made very often. In a world of change, of evolving opportunities and problems, adequate sectoral performance requires at the least that the sector respond to changing patterns of demand and cost, and that it seize new opportunities created outside the sector. One would hope that the sector would go beyond these minimal requirements and generate attractive new alternatives. This has been too little recognized in the intellectual traditions concerned with organizational choice. To a distressing degree, organizations are analyzed in terms of how well they do in a given situation or narrowly defined set of situations. Recently there has been a significant breaking away from this perspective in the organizational-administration literature. In economics there long has been smouldering argument between the neo-classicalists and the neo-Schumpeterians, with the former viewing the organizational problem in terms of maximization of social utility from given resources and technologies, and the latter proposing that what we really want of our organizations is rapid and well-directed innovation.[13] It is interesting that both

[13]See the discussion in R. Nelson, "Issues and Suggestions for the Study of Industrial Organization in a Regime of Rapid Technological Change," in V. Fuchs, ed., *Policy Issues and Research Opportunities in Industrial Organization* (New York: Columbia University Press, for the National Bureau of Economic Research, 1972).

camps have proposed a competitive, free-enterprise solution to the organizational problem, although there is disagreement on the meaning of "competitive" in that context. But consideration of the issues involved here leads us naturally to the third tradition mentioned earlier—science and technology policy.

4

THE ROLE OF KNOWLEDGE AND TECHNOLOGY

FROM STILL ANOTHER point of view, the moon-ghetto metaphor is about the way that scientific knowledge and technological capabilities have evolved in this country. It is not simply a matter of deciding to do a better job of education, or of air quality control, or of licking cancer—of scanning the alternatives and picking the best, and establishing the organization that will do the job. It can be argued that presently we don't know how, or lack the technology, to do greatly better in these areas, at least at an acceptable cost. The broad central premise of the science and technology policy perspective—that the range of available alternatives and our understanding of their consequences evolves as a result of our efforts to advance our knowledge and capabilities—now is shared by the two other intellectual traditions discussed above. The new emphasis on research, and the experimental philosophy of policy making, that increasingly characterize the policy analysis perspective, are quite comfortable. Similarly, an open-ended evolutionary perspective on the characteristics of good organizational performance cuts across the boundaries of the intellectual traditions.

Yet the science and technology policy perspective places the stress differently. Where the policy analysis perspective sees a chief executive making decisions, and the organizational perspective sees institutional structure as determining what is going on, the science and technology perspective focuses on the human intellectual enterprise, the human creativity and capability for learning and mastering nature, and sees the policy problem in terms of giving thrust and guidance to these forces.[1]

[1]This perception is there in Francis Bacon and Roger Bacon. The articulation that proved important in stimulating the post–World-War-II faith in science policy in the United States was V. Bush, *Science, The Endless Frontier* (Washington, D.C.: U.S. Government Printing Office, 1945). In England the seminar contemporary work probably was J. D. Bernal, *The Social Function of Science* (London: Routledge and Kegan Paul, 1939).

This perspective, like the others, is quite sweeping and can encompass almost anything. Additional intellectual commitments are necessary for it to have any real grip on policy. The key intellectual commitment is the focus on a particular kind of resource-manpower with advanced formal training in the basic and applied sciences, and its employment in a particular kind of activity—organized research or development consciously aimed at achieving certain kinds of knowledge or technological capabilities. This commitment effectively differentiates the science and technology perspective from the policy analysis perspective. While "advanced formal training in the basic and applied sciences" can be read as meaning "economists," this clearly is not the intent of the phrase; nor can "organized research and development" legitimately be read as "policy analysis." And the focus on organized R & D, with the implicit assumption of a degree of independence from other aspects of organization, rather sharply separates the science and technology perspective from the general organizational perspective.

These commitments are narrowing, but are necessary if the R & D allocation problem is to be posed in a persuasive manner. It might be argued that the nation's intellectual resources ought to be defined as including economists and other social scientists as well as natural scientists, possibly lawyers and skilled administrators (social engineers), and perhaps even bright and creative people generally. Similarly, it can be argued that much useful knowledge is gained and a considerable amount of technological and social invention take place outside of formal R & D activities, at least if these are narrowly defined; thus, one should interpret R & D broadly as including all human efforts at improving understanding or abilities in the areas under consideration. In many ways these arguments are very plausible. But if they are accepted, one loses any real grip on how to assess the current quantity and allocation of R & D efforts, and it becomes very difficult to think about how one can change the existing situation in various desired directions. In the nineteenth century, when it was widely believed that most important technological developments were the result of creative individuals, with no particular educational background, working alone, often part time, on problems that gripped them, it was virtually impossible to think of policies that would increase or reallocate inventive effort. In the mid-twentieth century, with the widely held belief that technical advance comes about from research and development done by scientists and engineers, it is possible to think about a range of policies for augmenting or reallocating R & D.

The science and technology policy tradition thus is based on the implicit hypothesis that a considerable share of the nation's problem-solving talent (in the areas of concern) has a specific kind of educational background and that the relevant advances come about through certain reasonably well defined activities (although the boundary lines are admittedly fuzzy). There is ample confirming evidence that this is so for certain fields like chemical and electronic products, aviation, atomic energy. But the basic tenet of the science and technology approach to the moon-ghetto problem is that these resources and activities are powerful across a wide range of problems, and that this range includes a large share of those we presently are interested in.

The Science of Science Policy

If the major factual premise is accepted, it is plausible to search for a resolution to the moon-ghetto problem in the reallocation of our R & D efforts. The policy problem then becomes to establish the criteria for reallocation, and to find policies that will make reallocation effective. But while, in many instances, the science and technology perspective provides a persuasive way of posing the problem, the tradition has been weak in setting forth normative criteria, and fractious and unpersuasive in proposing how to marshal science and technology to deal with the new problems. The "science of science policy" is very soft.

This basic softness of the R & D policy tradition is in good part the result of the fact that very few people have done serious analysis of social problems, a much smaller group than that associated with either of the two traditions considered earlier. The slimness of the intellectual foundations of science policy tends to get overlooked. It is too easy to move from the quite correct premise that physics is a more powerful discipline than economics or political science, to the non sequitur that we know how to apply physics to solve the problems of the world. Knowledge of how to marshal physics effectively to solve our problems (if indeed there is a way) is not the traditional subject matter of physics (and few physicists have given the matter much thought). A smattering of economists have concerned themselves with technical change and related policy issues, as have a few sociologists, political scientists, and historians; and a small but distinguished group of natural scientists have taken a serious and sustained intellectual interest in matters of science policy. But much of what they have accomplished is to chase the primary questions back to deeper ones, without providing solid knowledge that one confidently could use to guide policy.[2]

That much of science policy rests on intellectual quicksand has not deterred the evolution of a considerable R & D budget in government, and the development of a complex policy-making apparatus and organization. Until the late 1960s, fear of the Soviet Union, the emergence of exciting prospects in space, atomic energy, and biomedical technology, rising demands for higher education, and moderately persuasive arguments in favor of expanded support for basic research at the universities, sufficed to keep science well fed. And many of the accomplishments of the R & D system so constructed have been extremely impressive. But, in an era where these expansive forces have

[2]A good share of the more interesting articles on science policy have been published in the journal *Minerva*. For a sampler of articles from *Minerva*, see E. Shils, ed., *Criteria for Scientific Development* (Cambridge: M.I.T. Press, 1968). Among the classic books on science policy are D. K. Price, *Government and Science* (New York: New York University Press, 1964), and *The Scientific Estate* (Cambridge: Harvard University Press, 1965), H. Brooks, *The Government of Science* (Cambridge: M.I.T. Press, 1968); A. Weinberg, *Reflections on Big Science* (Cambridge: M.I.T. Press, 1967).

been damped and there is a sense of déjà vu about space, science and technology have been called upon to justify themselves in terms of their power to solve other national problems. The burdens on the intellectual structure have proved more than it could bear. There have been proposals for more or reallocated basic research, for big pushes (modeled after the space program) in areas of national need, for providing subsidies and incentives to industry, for technology assessment. But the arguments have not been persuasive, do not hang together, and are too readily dismissed as self serving.

We earlier saw the consequences of the lack of a coherent normative structure within a tradition. Economists and policy analysts walk in to fill the vacuum. The questions of the power of R & D as an instrument of attack can be posed in the language of policy analysis and, indeed, key members of the policy analysis community, entrenched in such places as the Office of Management and Budget, have been relatively successful in establishing their preferred language and criteria as a framework for thinking about this question. From this perspective, the debate about the appropriate level and allocation of government R & D spending should be treated like any other question for rational policy analysis. One can pose the question of the efficacy of R & D as an instrument of attack on a problem in terms of its rate of return compared with other instruments. If, given an appropriate valuation of what we want to achieve, R & D has a high rate of return, it is an attractive instrument. A high rate of return on R & D is likely if there are valuable objectives that cannot be achieved (or are very costly to achieve) with existing knowledge and technology, and if R & D has a good chance of success in making these objectives achievable.

Our problems clearly differ significantly in the extent to which we presently have the knowledge and technology to achieve, at reasonable cost, a significant improvement in the situation. Garbage on the streets of New York, or the miserable quality of passenger rail service, certainly can be significantly ameliorated without any major advance in scientific knowledge, or any new engineering systems. This is not to say that better knowledge and systems might not help. But absence of better technology cannot be regarded as the present constraint. On the other hand, we really do not know how to significantly reduce deaths from certain kinds of cancer. While we know how to achieve higher levels of air pollution control, the costs (in terms of resources or inconvenience or both) are enormous if we aim for large quality improvements in urban areas. And there are reasons to doubt that we presently have the knowledge or technique to greatly increase effectiveness of teaching of reading to ghetto kids, or significantly reduce drug addiction, or crime in the streets.

But efficacy of R & D as a policy instrument requires more than that the results if achieved be valuable. R & D must have promise of achieving these results at reasonable cost. Here we come back to a problem posed earlier. While formally trained scientists and engineers, engaged in organized R & D, have been remarkably effective in advancing knowledge and creating powerful new capabilities in certain selected arenas, there is a strong element of faith attached to the proposition that these kinds of talents and activities can be applied powerfully to the solution of almost any problem. It seems like a good bet that conventionally trained scientists and engineers, doing R & D of the traditional sort, can make a good deal of headway against the pollution problem. But it would appear that many of the problems of the inner city are not amenable to attack by science and technology of the traditional kind. Our ability to deal with problems of crime and education certainly is limited by our existing knowledge and techniques. Though one can give some counterarguments, it does not seem that these problems can be readily attacked through the traditional natural sciences, nor is it easy to envisage hardware that engineers can design that will make much of a real dent.[3]

[3]For an exploration of the feasibility of traditional science and technology solutions to certain problems, see A. Etzioni and R. Remp, *Technological Shortcuts to Social Change* (New York: Russell Sage Foundation, 1973).

The intellectual traditions considered earlier have developed their own research agenda of hard questions, and are in a strong position for arguing that these are more germane to the problems of the day than the traditional kinds of questions asked by natural scientists and technologists. The key questions that have hampered the capabilities of the policy analysis and organizational reform traditions originate in the social sciences, not the natural sciences. But a problem is that the behavioral and social sciences have not been as powerful as the natural sciences. Tension therefore exists between the natural and social science communities about how the redirected R & D enterprise should go. The natural scientists have reacted to their perception of the limited progress made by social scientists by, in effect, proposing that the natural scientists and engineers should move in and take over the fields. However, early efforts by natural scientists to till the social science fields have not, to say the least, been very promising.[4]

One possibility is that these kinds of problems are simply intractable. Another possibility—the one on which many scientists (both natural and social) would place their bets—is that what is needed is significant advances in scientific methodology (for example, methods of social experimentation), and that this is achieveable with enough effort and time. Still another possibility is that the understanding and technique will evolve, but it will evolve through the experience and sharpened imagination of people who are actually trying to deal with the problems, not through the data gathering and theorizing of people with fancy degrees doing something called research or development.

The research and development policy tradition may justly be accused of a certain elitism regarding the nation's problem-solving endeavors. For millennia, humans have made intellectual and technological progress without much in the way of organized science, and in many fields today this still is the case.

---

[4]A striking example of work by a natural scientist in the social science arena is J. Forrester, *World Dynamics* (Cambridge, Mass.: Wright-Allen Press, 1971). The argument was extended and popularized in D. L. Meadows, et al., *The Limits of Growth* (New York: Signet Books, 1972). For complaints and rejoinders from social scientists see the entire April 1973 issue of *Futures*.

The advocate of R & D might reply, appropriately, that the pace of progress has been much greater where scientific knowledge has been brought to bear, and that the R & D instrument has the advantage of manipulability. The skeptic might reply that all that is true, but there are good reasons for keeping the size of the formal R & D bets limited until formal R & D has proved itself.

The Governance of Science

The question of how effectively to reallocate R & D is as basic to the development of an effective science policy as the question of whether, if resources were effectively reallocated, the returns would be high. Nor can the two questions be easily separated. The rate of return on R & D is not simply determined by the quantity of resources allocated to a job. It depends, as well, on how the broad mandate is interpreted, on what strategy is adopted, how the detailed decisions are made, and how the work is carried out. These, as well extrinsic factors, will determine what actually will be achieved.

Thus perhaps the most fundamental R & D policy questions are those regarding organization and governance. There has been considerable disarray within the R & D community regarding these questions. It seems fair to say, however, that behind the scenes there are two widely shared premises. The first is that the output, the benefits, of R & D are often quite widespread in their impact—and hence cannot (and should not) be treated as private goods, but rather must be treated as public goods. Thus, R & D needs public support. The second premise is that to a considerable extent the scientific community itself should decide what areas and strategies are most promising, subject to quite broad guidelines regarding the practical dimensions of the public interest.[5] But there is lack of

[5]For a general review, see R. Nelson, M. J. Peck, and E. P. Kalachek, *Technology, Economic Growth and Public Policy* (Washington, D.C.: Brookings Institution, 1967).

consensus, to say the least, about the desire of publicness of various kinds of R & D activity, and about how scientific judgment and the public interest in certain kinds of outcomes are to be blended into an effective governing structure. And as we saw earlier, this hesitant situation is ripe for intellectual imperialism by economists.

There has been greater than average agreement within the science and technology policy community regarding academic basic research, and unlike other areas of R & D policy, economists have tended to go along with the arguments regarding the publicness of the benefits of basic research. In addition to the consensus that the "public" qualities of the knowledge won through basic research call for public financing, there is widespread agreement that the scientific community itself should play a large role in guiding the allocation of basic research resources according to criteria that stress scientific promise.[6] The same attributes that make it sensible to support basic research as a public good—great ex ante uncertainty regarding the nature and scope of the payoff and considerable if often diffuse ex post range of applicability—mean that it is important to guard the basic research allocation decisions against the undue interjection of criteria relating to specific economic or social payoffs.

But there is considerable room for disagreement regarding the meaning of "large" and "undue." There is tension between those who stress the importance of an autonomous "Republic of Science" and those who emphasize that considerations of social and economic value and cost, judged in considerable part by nonscientists, should play a major role in determining basic research allocation decisions. The controversies here shade over into a semantically adjacent area—the relative emphasis that should be placed on basic versus applied research.

The dispute involving the National Institutes of Health and

[6]Perhaps the best-articulated argument for self-governance of science is by Michael Polanyi: "The Republic of Science," *Minerva*, Autumn 1962 (reprinted in Shils, *Criteria for Scientific Development*).

the War on Cancer is an excellent case in point. Here, one side of the debate insists that the objective of better health can be won more efficiently if, and perhaps only if, the strategy involves, at least at its early stage, a heavy emphasis on basic research. Further, this side argues that the basic research funding should be guided largely by the scientific interest and merit of the proposals, which criteria must be judged by the relevant scientific community. The counterargument is that a decision to place high priority on licking cancer (implying a lower priority for other disease categories) provides a criterion that must and can be weighed along with scientific merit in judging alternative ways to spend research monies. This position emphasizes that an efficient program of research on cancer requires a considerable degree of overall planning, targeting, and coordination of research projects. And, in contrast with a strategy that stresses basic research—where university scientists would be the natural "doers"—the strategy emphasizing a planned attack is associated with significant use of government labs and contracts with business.[7]

The key issues here—the extent to which social and economic criteria should be weighed explicitly in determining research allocation, and the way in which research program ought to be managed and organized—captures the essence of the debate about the appropriate mix between "basic" and "applied" research. Of these two issues, the governance issue is by far the more important. It is only through governance that criteria are applied and enforced. Given that it is agreed that a particular research program ought to be guided by certain criteria of social and economic merit, rather than solely criteria of scientific interest, to what extent does the argument for autonomy from routine governance, accededly applicable to basic research, also apply here?

Many natural scientists and engineers apparently take the point of view that applied research, like basic research, re-

---

[7]See, for example, S. Strickland, "Integration of Medical Research and Health Policies," *Science*, September 1971.

quires a considerable amount of autonomy.[8] A "public good" or "externality" argument is implicit, and usually associated with assertions about the short time horizons, narrow incentives, and limited range of perceptions of business people and public officials. Further, the argument goes, technical people, not private or public bureaucrats of a traditional stripe, ought to guide the program. The relatively high degree of autonomy, for instance, which the National Institutes in fact achieved during the 1960s in their dealings with HEW as well as with the White House and with Congress, is deemed to be a very desirable thing. Agencies like the old Atomic Energy Commission, and NASA, which were largely defined in terms of R & D, are considered good organizational models.

While to the natural scientist considerable autonomy for applied science, as well as for basic science, seems a natural desideratum, economists tend to view the matter quite otherwise. Focusing as they have on R & D done in industry, they see applied R & D as an activity carried out, to a considerable extent, by firms in the sector under consideration, induced by the framework of incentives bearing on those firms, and built into the general organization of the sector. Economists tend to downplay externality arguments in the context of applied R & D. Viewing applied R & D as much like any other kind of investment made by an organization, their theoretical preconceptions lead them to worry when they see R & D activity going on with only tenuous connections with the demand-articulating mechanisms, and the supply organization, of the sector. Should not R & D priorities be set by, or be responsive to, the mechanisms that determine the "worth" of various outputs of the sector? If values are adequately expressed as incentives, does it not make sense to delegate R & D decision making to the "supplying" organization? By and large, economists have been suspicious of a separate "governance" of R & D. Rather, they

---

[8]The following characterization of views reflects the author's own impressions gleaned from many unpublished discussions and debates. There does not seem to be a good compact reference.

see the objective as somehow getting the R & D machinery built into the general governing machinery of the sector.

Many natural scientists, concerned with R & D policy, have found the economists' perspective hard to swallow. There are several reasons. It can be argued that economists vastly overstate the extent to which profit incentives (or the self-interest and judgment of government officials) can "pull" the applied R & D that has high social payoff; the cases of myopia or significant externality that economists see as exceptions are, rather, the rule.

At a different level of argument, the case for controlling applied science subsuming it under the more general apparatus of sectoral governance hinges on the argument that the overall governing structure is adequate. But if there is any merit to the criticism that in many of the problem sectors the overall organization is not working well, this argument begs the question. In some cases one can see that patching up the value-articulation mechanism, or the supply mechanism, might go a long way toward providing more appropriate guidance to R & D. One might motivate more private R & D on pollution control through establishment of a system of pollution charges, with government R & D funds going into basic and exploratory work. Freeing passenger rail supply of many of its regulatory constraints and encouraging more concern for profit might well pull a more creative and effective R & D effort out of the railroad industry and rail suppliers. But how to obtain better demand and supply machinery in education, medical care, criminal justice, is not easy to see. And until that organizational problem is resolved, the economists' argument that a smoothly working sectoral command and control system will induce R & D begs the question.

There certainly is merit in the thesis that in many of these cases if more R & D is to be done, and allocated sensibly, public funds and direction are needed. But implicitly this position raises a larger issue. If economists can justly be accused both of ignoring special R & D governing structures in their consideration of problems of economic organization and of taking the simple-minded position that markets can and do effectively solve most of our problems of overall sectoral governance, the R & D policy analysis tradition can justly be accused of being fuzzy and schizophrenic regarding the relationship between R & D and overall sectoral governance. On the one hand, there has been an implicit faith that if the R & D machinery generates a "solution," the solution will be adopted. On the other hand, there has been a deep mistrust in the current governing and organization of many of our sectors, particularly the market sectors. But if one takes the position that the overall governing structure of a sector is inadequate, special governance of R & D will not help very much. For it is the higher-order structure that determines which of the scientists' creations will, and will not, be employed. If a separate "Republic of Science" notion is only marginally viable for basic research, it clearly is absurd for applied research. There must be close linkage between research and applications.

The R & D policy community increasingly has come to recognize this. The discussion has developed along two quite different lines. One of them is concerned with identifying the obstacles to innovation in various sectors, and with scanning the wide list of governmental policies that could be used to stimulate innovation. The resulting broadening of the list of possible policy instruments, and the focusing on methods for indirectly stimulating R & D, has established more of a bridge between the R & D policy community and general economists. However, a secondary quarrel has developed about the emphasis to be placed on the R & D impact of a policy, compared with its other effects. Thus, proposals that R & D be granted tax credits conflict with notions that our tax structure is already too complex. The argument that certain cooperative R & D projects are being deterred by the antitrust laws is countered by the position that the overriding purpose of antitrust policy is to try to preserve competitive structure, and that the occasional deterrence of a worthwhile research endeavor is not much of a cost.

The second line of discussion is concerned that in many

cases the problem with the overall sectoral governing structure is not that it is too rigid, but that it does not adequately discriminate between desirable and undesirable innovations. The R & D policy community has begun to adopt the perspective of many sociologists and historians that the very process of technological change itself is a major reason for the inadequacies of our governing structures. According to this perspective, our economic and social institutions are designed to govern particular regimes of technology, and when faced with rapid and significant technological change are unable effectively to screen the good from the bad, or to make the most of the new alternatives that are available.

The idea, and the practice, of government screening technology is not new. The FDA has a long and controversial history, and the issues surrounding its policies long anticipated the current debates about the Consumer Product Safety Commission and the Council on Environmental Quality. Clearly, technology assessment is a complex matter. Several recent reports have discussed the issues in a sophisticated and illuminating manner.[9]

But behind the sophisticated dialogue, the old fractious stylized argument between economist and natural scientist drones on. Many an economist sees the whole discussion as basically misconceived. In the first place, economists see the current regime of sectoral governance as serving the "traffic cop" role in a reasonably effective way. But, more basically, they do not see how technology assessment is supposed to work, who is to overrule the market on the basis of what criteria, how complaints and warnings are to be judged and made effective, and so forth.

On the other hand, many natural scientists see technology assessment as a way to right the old wrongs of an unplanned, greed-driven, capitalist system. The idea of "technology as-

[9]See, in particular, *Technology: Processes of Assessment and Choice*, Report of the National Academy of Sciences to the House Committee on Science and Astronautics, July 1969.

sessment" is, of course, only the latest wrinkle in the more general idea that scientists and engineers should play a much larger role in governing the nation, a role that goes far beyond deciding what R & D should be done. In many ways, many natural scientists' perception of how the political economy ought to be run is strikingly reminiscent of the economists' early perception of the role of the policy analyst. And all of the problems that were latent in that position are latent in the scientists' notion of the desirability of rule by scientific advisers. So we return to square one and Plato's philosopher-king (or the king's council).

5

THE CURRENT
INTELLECTUAL MALAISE

Each of the intellectual traditions we have considered sheds some light. But each is in difficulty and flux. It is hard to believe that they have enabled us fully to exploit the room for maneuver between the Scylla of political intransigency and the Charybdis of the technically infeasible. Part of the difficulty certainly resides in lack of basic knowledge of what will and will not work. Indeed, one could read this essay as simple advocacy for more research in the social and behavioral sciences. But my intended thrust is in another direction. Our ability to deal with many of our problems has been at least as much limited by the clumsiness of the analysis as by any basic lack of knowledge. And the clumsiness has been in large part due to insensitivity to the limitations of intellectual structures.

All the traditions possess an enormous amount of confidence that it is possible to find technically correct answers to important policy problems; they play down or ignore that many problems may be largely political, involving real conflicts of interest that cannot be dissolved by sweet rationalism. Other traditions of problem solving or analysis recognize conflict much more explicitly. The legal perspective, for example, is largely oriented around ways to avoid or resolve conflict. Marxians differentiated themselves from Utopian socialists by their explicit recognition of conflict. But implicitly the faith of the three traditions of analysis discussed here is that for many problems this is possible. The connotation of "a technically correct solution" is that in the long run, solutions of the "correct" form make everyone better off. It is somewhat surprising, therefore, that all three traditions have been relatively blind to exactly the kind of disagreements, and conflicting interests, which need to be perceived in order to guide search for solutions that, over the long run, do not harm significant values or groups. Recently there have been promising signs of enhanced political sensitivity among analysts of all schools. This should help.

It also would help if analysts had a little less self-confidence, and did a little less overselling, regarding the scientific basis of the prescriptions they offer. Analytic structures are powerful devices for focusing knowledge on a problem. However, it has proved easy to confuse form with substance; on too many occasions, arguments that sounded rigorous but had little supporting evidence have carried undue weight. Scientism has been frequent in part because of lack of awareness of how weak our knowledge in the social and behavioral sciences really is. But in good part scientism has crept in because of a failure to see beneath the logical sharpness of a normative argument to the empirical weaknesses of the factual premises on which the real cut of that argument depends.

Experience within each of the three perspectives suggests that the attention of the analyst is pulled toward those parts of the intellectual frame that have a strong normative structure: that is, a clear characterization of interesting alternatives and clear criteria (or rationalizations) for choice. It is here that the economists' tools have proved their mettle. Armed with the clear-cut concepts of the logic of choice and the calculational structure of cost-benefit analysis, the economists took over the policy analysis tradition. Equipped with the powerful and elegant model of how market-organized economies operate and with arguments for their optimality, the economists' perspective has dominated the search for organizational solutions. And economists have played an increasingly important role in policy deliberations about science and technology. The rigor of their normative arguments has tended to bedazzle the eyes, and to take attention away from the shakiness of their predictions about how various policies and organizational arrangements in fact would work.

There has been some check on scientism. Occasionally, this check has been quite explicit: particular predictions lying behind particular prescriptions have been observed to be wrong. More commonly, the check has been implicit and indirect. Arguments taking the form of scientific statements ultimately are vulnerable to a variety of evidence in rebuttal. Thus the policy analysts were vulnerable to the arguments that they had incorrectly modeled the "educational production function," advocates of more competition in education had to respond to the criticism that their case was based on a model of economic activity which did not fit education, and advocates of solving the educational problem by engineering R & D were faced with a variety of arguments about the limited utility of teaching machines. But the slowness of this process and the support often given to the form rather than the substance of scientific argument are a bit disturbing.

There seems little doubt that a good deal of the analytical clumsiness stems from the rather remarkable parochialism that has marked the separate intellectual traditions. Each provides, at one level, a great sweeping framework that is broad enough to encompass almost anything. And the high practitioners of the different traditions often talk as if theirs were a master perspective. But to be helpful in actually characterizing policy problems, the structures are forced to make some severe intellectual commitments that, upon reflection, are seen to drastically narrow their scope. Thus the policy analysis perspective is tied to the image of a chief executive making decisions, the organization perspective highlights institutional structure, the science and technology perspective focuses on the allocation of R & D resources. Once these commitments are recognized, it becomes possible to ask seriously whether one perspective, or another, or any of them really characterizes a particular problem in an illuminating way. However, progress in delineating the real problem has been handicapped by the reluctance of the separate traditions to recognize the limits of their own domains.

Recognition of limitations of each of the frameworks would be an important step forward. I see no magic in an integrated perspective. A framework of appreciation that tries to encompass everything will end up effectively encompassing nothing. Each of the three traditions provides a plausible way of looking at a wide class of problems. For some problems the different perspectives seem to complement each other nicely by pointing each to a different facet. Much of what is needed is the sharpening up of the separate perspectives.

However, I see nothing particularly sacred in the particular perspectives around which the main traditions have clustered. It would be sheer luck if all problems were well fit by one of the analytic wrenches, or by some combination of them. And indeed there seem to be a number of important problems that none of the traditions really seem to grasp. Different ways of looking at problems would seem to be in order. In attempting to deal with problems of education, medical care, pollution, the practitioners of each of the traditions has been forced by the anatomy of the problem to go beyond the boundaries of their traditions. In many cases their search for a useful way of analyzing the problem has led them into portions of the traditional terrain of other disciplines. However, the encounters in the borderland have tended to be fractious. Each of the traditions has certain of the attributes of a religion. When those who profess their faiths have been found venturing into a different tradition, they have been treated as heathen.

Often the intellectual costs have been great. Because they would not or could not absorb what has been learned by the unanointed, the practitioners' policy proposals have been unnecessarily unpersuasive, or demonstrably inadequate. The symptoms, and the consequences, have been Babel. The retreat of the modern policy analysts might have been more orderly and better directed toward reestablishing terrain, if that tradition had better absorbed the wisdom of public administration. The frustration of current science policy in good part reflects the inability of policy analysts, and those who have thought long and hard about science policy, effectively to communicate with each other. In some cases simple open-minded communication would have an enormously salutary effect. In other cases the problem is more severe, and a truly integrated perspective will need to be built; but a start on that problem also requires more in the way of open-minded communication.

I have some rather strong beliefs about the kinds of analyses that are most needed. While these are implicit in what has gone before, it is time now to make them explicit and to pull them together into a coherent perception.

While the language of choice and decision has a certain appeal, and presidents and other chief executives have a great deal of power, I suspect that further elaboration of the policy analysis metaphor as it traditionally has been structured will provide very low marginal returns in terms of extending the range of problems to which the framework is applicable. But two key intellectual developments within that tradition do promise an extension of range: the recognition of the saliency of organizational structure, and the recognition of the open-ended evolutionary way in which policies and programs do and should unfold. These developments call for rather sharp shifts in intellectual focus, carrying the analysis outside the traditional language and terrain.

To extend the range of problems we can analyze in an illuminating way, we must overhaul and enrich the way we characterize and analyze organizational alternatives, for in many of the most important policy arenas these define the real domain of choice. An important number of our policy problems call for the design of complex institutional structures, and defy being pressed into one or another of the small set of stylized organizational alternatives modeled by economists and other social scientists.

It also is of high priority that we become much more sophisticated regarding the processes by which new knowledge and technolgies evolve, and the policies that will further these processes. Questions of stimulation and control, of science and technology are extremely important in many economic sectors, and are the central issues in some.

For some policy issues I suspect that effective analysis

requires a synthesis of the organizational and evolutionary views of things. Our major complaints about many of our problem sectors and activities are that, on the one hand, they have not responded adequately to significant changes in the nature of demand and supply conditions imposed upon them, and that on the other, they have not been able effectively to bring forth or adapt the possibilities latent in advancing general science, in technology created in other sectors, and in other developments. A given organizational frame may be adequate to meet our wants and exploit the opportunities under some demand and supply regimes, but not others. Organizational structures that once were adequate may be made inadequate by changes external to the sector. Or the changes may be internal; the organization of a sector may become obsolete through its own dynamics. High-level policy problems arise as the result of such changes.

These commitments are somewhat abstract. In the following two chapters I shall try to make them more substantive and concrete by considering in detail two recent policy dialogues, the first concerned with the role of the federal government in the provision of extrafamily care for young children, the second the issue of federal support for the development of a supersonic transport and the liquid metal breeder reactor. In reading each study, the reader should be alert that the focus is narrowed not merely because specific cases are being discussed, but also because I am taking a particular perspective on problems and possible solutions. In each case the focus will be organizational, and in each the analysis will hinge on characterization of changing conditions. This perspective is not the only one that can be applied to these problems, but my argument is that it is a very useful one. In the concluding chapter I will explore some of the common elements in these case studies, looking at the general problem of the governance of economic activity in a world of change.

6

PUBLIC POLICY AND THE ORGANIZATION OF DAY CARE FOR YOUNG CHILDREN

WHILE THE public policy debate over day care has tended to define the problem as one of funding, that is as an "investment" problem. I propose that the problem essentially is organizational. The policy issue has arisen because of deep-seated changes in the structure of the American economy that are making increasingly problematic for many families the traditional mode for care of young children—the adult female of the family staying home with the child. While the pressures for the generation of organizational alternatives are obvious, the nature of a satisfactory alternative is far from clear.

Day care is an activity for which none of the standard organizational categories seems appropriate, and hence is requiring of sophisticated organizational design. But because the organizational aspects of the problem have not been recognized, there in fact has been very little serious organizational thinking. Many other problems are like day care in these respects, involving complex organizational issues that defy simple solutions, and a policy dialogue that fails to recognize this adequately.

The Demand for Extrafamily Day Care

The Prevalence of Child Care in the Home / Child care is a striking example of an activity whose prevalent mode of organization and governance has been different from the forms most studied by economists and political scientists. The resources involved are enormous.[1] Assume that child care was pur-

[1]Despite the general parochialism, several studies deal with these topics, and to these this study is indebted—e.g., K. J. Arrow, in his "Uncertainty and

chased by parents. In 1976 there were roughly 18 million
American children under five years old. Existing federal day
care standards require a minimum of one adult for every five
children, or more than 3.5 million adults—double the number
of teachers presently in our public schools. Even at a ratio of
one adult for eight children (roughly the average in day-care
centers), with a mean annual salary of $6,000 per day-care
worker (again about average) and total costs of about 1.3 times
salary cost, the bill would amount to $18 billion a year.[2]

Of course, most child care is not transacted for by parents
but is undertaken by the parents themselves. But the fact that
no money changes hands in quid-pro-quo transactions means
merely that the total does not show up in GNP accounts; the
resources are no less real. The interesting issue is why most
families have chosen to care for their own children rather than
purchasing child care from others.

Obviously there are "preference" or "consumption" factors.
Most families gain satisfaction out of caring for their own
children—a not unmixed blessing, but still for many mothers a
more attractive occupation than most available forms of employment for money. Social attitudes about what is best for
the child, about the duties of mothers to their children, and
about the proper economic role of women certainly have reinforced this factor. Nor are there compelling "efficiencies" from
specialization and trade. While there are some economies of
scale in child care, these are far less important than in many

the Economics of Medical Care," *American Economic Review,* December
1963, developed a provocative discussion of nonprofit organizations. Several
economists have considered the family, e.g., J. Mincer, "Labor Force Participation of Married Women: A Study of Labor Supply," in National Bureau of
Economic Research, *Aspects of Labor Economics* (Princeton: Princeton University Press, 1967), and G. Becker, "A Theory of the Allocation of Time,"
Economic Journal, September 1965.

[2]Basic data are from *Day Care Survey of 1970* (Washington, D.C.: West-
inghouse Learning Corporation for the Office of Economic Opportunity, 1972).
Henceforth, this study will be referred to as the Westinghouse Study. The
Office of Child Development recommends a day-care program that costs
roughly three times this figure. For a discussion of day costs per child, see D.
Young and R. R. Nelson, *Public Policy for Day Care of Young Children*
(Lexington, Mass.: Lexington Books, 1973).

other activities, and specific training is not generally regarded as essential to good child care. Furthermore, as long as other activities are going on in the household—cleaning, cooking, or specialized economic activity for sale on the market, such as working on the family farm—the extra time cost of looking after children is less than it would be for an organization specializing in child care.

Finally, and of major importance when considering modes of extrafamily child care, there are questions of effective control of the way children are cared for. Parents may be wary of entrusting the care of their children to outsiders who may be fast-buck artists with no real concern for children's welfare, or may be incompetent, or may pursue goals in child rearing that run counter to those of the parents. The question of trust and confidence in judgment is a central issue in the care of one's children, and can best be resolved by doing it oneself.

Factors Affecting Demand for Extrafamily Child Care / Obviously these factors have not been powerful enough to keep child care strictly within the family. Their force, and hence the demand for extrafamily child-care services, depends on a number of variables, some characteristic of the family, some of the state of the economy, some attitudinal. Trends in demographic and economic structure, as well as attitudinal changes, appear to have worked in the direction of increasing the demand for extrafamily day care.

The decline in mortality rates over the years, both for children and adults, has resulted in significant changes in American family characteristics. While there undoubtedly has been a significant long-run decline in family goals regarding the number of surviving children, there is no hard evidence to prove this. However, even given a constant family-size goal, the dramatic decline in child death rates achieved over the last half century would have led to a decline in the number of desired births and young children per family.[3] In 1900, mortal-

---

[3]T. P. Schultz, "An Economic Model of Family Planning and Fertility," *Journal of Political Economy* 77 (March–April 1969).

ity for children under one year was 162 per thousand; by 1950, it was under 30 per thousand. The death rate for children one through four years has fallen from 19 per thousand in 1900, to 2.9 in 1949, and to about 1.1 by the late 1950s, since which time it has remained essentially stable. Birth rates have fallen in compensation. The results of these trends have been a significant, if somewhat erratic, long-run decline in the number of children under five per women twenty to forty-four years old: the figure was 1.3 in 1800, around 0.7 or 0.8 in 1900, declined to 0.4 in 1940, increased in the postwar years, and fell to 0.35 in 1970.

In a related development, the median age of wives at the birth of the last child has declined from the late thirties around 1800 to the early thirties in 1900 and to the late twenties today.[4] Over the same period, the life expectancy of women at age twenty has risen by twenty years, by ten since 1900. With a decline in the age where childbearing is complete and an increase in life expectancy, a significant number of years now remain to most women after their child-rearing tasks have become minimal, something that was still far from the rule in the early twentieth century.[5]

These demographic developments have strengthened the economic rationale for extrafamily day care. For families with three or more young children, the economies of extrafamily day care are likely to be small. If the children stay at home, the mother is pretty well occupied in their care plus other activities around the house. If she sends them to outside day care, she is relieved, but someone else must do a comparable amount of work.[6] And other costs are involved in specialized day care.

[4] The mortality figures and the data on children per women are taken from *Historial Statistics of the United States* and the *Statistical Abstracts of the United States* (Washington, D.C.: U.S. Government Printing Office, 1972).

[5] See R. Wells, "Demographic Change in the Life Cycle for American Families from the 18th to 20th Centuries," paper presented at the Population Association of America meeting of April 23, 1971, Washington, D.C.

[6] This analysis is implicit in G. Steiner, *The State of Welfare* (Washington, D.C.: Brookings Institution, 1971). It is virtually certain that a national program of subsidized day care would involve annual costs well over $1,000 per child, far above the $650 average reported in the Westinghouse Study.

While home space can be used for in-home day care, special facilities may be needed for care outside the home. When only one or two children are involved, however, potential economies of "specialization" begin to become substantial, and day care becomes a more attractive economic proposition. The increase in the number of years left to a woman after child-care responsibilities have become minimal also has worked in this direction. A longer expected potential working life justifies investment in future earning power. Completing college, or taking graduate work or professional training, which might not be a good investment if time horizons are short, may be well worth the investment when time horizons are longer. Part of that investment may be in day care for the young children.

Not only demographic but also economic developments have acted to increase the demand for extrafamily day care. Not much more than a century ago, many families took care of a large fraction of their needs through their own activities, with "trading" much more limited than today. Even specialized and traded activities, like cash-crop farming or blacksmithing, often took place at or close to the home. The stable rural or small town environment tended to keep extended families in proximity. Today, home spinning and weaving don't make much economic sense, and if women are to earn a cash income they are likely to have to leave the daytime household. And neither father nor grandparents are likely to be around to babysit.

These factors certainly have been the principal causes of the rise in workforce participation of married women—from 5 percent in 1890 to 30 percent in 1960 to 40 percent in 1970. Participation rates for women with children under six increased from 12 percent in 1950 to 19 percent in 1960 to 28 percent in 1969.[7] While these figures probably overstate what has actually happened (in 1890 a larger fraction of married women worked on the family farm or along with their husbands, which factor is not adequately reflected in the 5 percent figure), the increase has been dramatic.

[7]*Statistical Abstract.*

There are some interesting questions about whether attitudinal changes are independent of, or actually rationalize,
changes in economic circumstance. However, there is no doubt
that the vast increases in female workforce participation have
been associated with changes in attitudes toward careers of
women.

Public Subsidy of Day Care / Almost all societies have expressed concern about the care and upbringing of young children, and child care never has been purely a matter of family
responsibility. There has been a long if erratic public involvement in the day care of preschool-age children. Under settle-
ment house and similar auspices, day care has been provided
for children of poor families where both or the only parent had
to work. During the heavy wave of immigration, day-care
nurseries were viewed by many Americans as a vehicle for
acculturating the children of poor immigrants—in effect, a way
of compensating for what was believed to be the poor upbringing such children got from their own parents. Day care traditionally has been a form of assistance advocated by social work-
ers for the treatment of troubled families.[8]

Since 1960 there has been a significant increase in federal
funding.[9] Public programs, by and large, have not operated
directly on supply but have supplemented private demand by
paying for day-care services provided under private (generally
nonprofit) auspices. There have been two principal rationales
behind the increase in public demand: one is the belief that
mothers of families on welfare ought to go to work to gain family
income; and the second is that children of poor and generally
minority group families (blacks, chicanos) would benefit from
the experience that can be provided in day-care centers compared to what they would receive within their families. Based
on these arguments, federal funds for day care rose from less
than $10 million in the early 1960s to $222 million in 1970. In

[8]For an excellent discussion of the history of day care, see G. Fein and
A. Clarke-Stewart, *Day Care in Context* (New York: John Wiley & Sons, 1973).

[9]For a more detailed account, see Steiner, *The State of Welfare*, and
Young and Nelson, *Public Policy for Day Care*.

1970, approximately 250,000 children received at least some subsidy under federal programs.

As with the increased private demand for extrafamily child care, government subsidy is undoubtedly here to stay and probably will grow significantly. However, the key driving force is unlikely to be the argument for day-care subsidy as a substitute for welfare payments. While there will likely be periodic flurries of such proposals, the case for day care on these grounds is simply very weak. Day care as a substitute for welfare makes sense when the mother is capable of earning good money, and there are only one or two children; this situation obtains in only a small portion of welfare cases. When these conditions do not obtain, a policy of forcing mothers to work and giving their children minimal day care may save public money, but at the expense of reducing the welfare of the children. While vindictiveness toward welfare mothers may be a powerful political force, evidence that a public program is hurting little children is likely to be political poison. On the other hand, if relatively high levels of day-care expenditure per child are contemplated, for many families public cost will be increased if the mother is compelled to work.[10] Unless there are positive benefits to children from day care, it doesn't make economic sense to force mothers with several young children into the job market. A simple income support check appears to be a far better policy.

The "benefits to children" rationale is intellectually more persuasive and likely to carry increasingly more political weight, particularly if it is integrated (as it surely will be) with arguments about the value of making it easier and cheaper for women who want to work to find suitable places to care for their children. There is ample evidence of the appalling conditions under which many poor working mothers leave their children, and a persuasive case can be made for remedial public-policy action. The argument, however, for the positive developmental

---

[10]There seems no point in working out the details of a cost-benefit analysis here. For various calculations, see Steiner, *The State of Welfare.*

advantages of day care for children where care is available at home has not been sufficiently persuasive to call forth a policy of general subsidy, justified on child benefit alone. This leads to the question of how to subsidize day care for children whose parents are already working, without providing an incentive for other parents to go to work and leave their children in subsidized day care. But this conundrum can be resolved by an explicit alliance with those who argue the importance of making it easier for mothers to find good places for their children if they want to work outside the home. New federal programs seem a good bet.

The Organization of Extrafamily Day Care

To a very considerable extent, the organization of nonsubsidized day care involves relatively informal arrangements —help through the extended family, or cottage industry. Of the children of full and part-time working mothers sampled in one study,[11] 80 percent were cared for by someone else in the family. For children of full-time working mothers, the figure was 53 percent. Similarly, a study of day care in the Washington, D.C. Model Neighborhood shows that 67 percent of the children of working mothers (full or part time) were cared for by a family member of the child's home, 19 percent of them in the relative's home.[12] In 10 percent of the cases, the supplier was labeled a babysitter who either came to the child's house or cared for the child in her own home. This "sitter" category undoubtedly overlaps the "family day-care home" category of the Westinghouse Study, in which roughly 850,000 children were found to be cared for in outside homes in which one or more sitters looked after one to six children.

[11] F. Low and T. Spindler, *Child Care Arrangement of Working Mothers in the United States* (U.S. Department of Health, Education, and Welfare, Children's Bureau Publication No. 461, 1968).

[12] R. Zamoff and L. Vogt, *Assessment of Day Care Services and Needs at the Community Level* (Washington, D.C.: Urban Institute, 1971).

A portion of nonsubsidized day care, but virtually all of subsidized day care, is undertaken in more formal, and generally larger organizations, for which the term "day-care centers" customarily is reserved. Steiner reports that the number of day-care centers tripled between 1960 and 1969.[13] The Westinghouse Study, using somewhat different definitions, reports 17,500 centers in 1970 offering day care for seven or more children, looking after 575,000 children on a full-day basis and after additional children part time. Sixty percent of the centers were proprietary; these accounted for about half of the children in day-care centers and received little subsidy. Most of the rest were nonproprietary; a small fraction were government operated. Many facilities were associated with community action agencies, and a few were run by public schools or state welfare departments. These nonproprietary and public centers were the principal beneficiaries of subsidies. Many provide quite elaborate day care, charging the parents less or at least no more than the proprietary centers.

While the circumstances have varied, depending on the nature of the legislation providing the subsidy (several agencies and programs were involved) and the policies of the local administrating agency, in many cases children eligible for day-care subsidy have no choice among centers. While "consumer sovereignty" is stressed in nongovernmental organizations, there seems to have been no intention of letting it play any role in monitoring the regime of subsidized day-care supply. This task has been left to the local government agencies providing the funds (welfare departments, community action or model cities organizations), to regulatory agencies (to monitor safety and space standards, etc.), and to chance.

It is widely agreed that this system has not worked very well. While most of the loud policy noise has been about the alleged need for more public funds, it is apparent that the existing supply of day care is often of shameful quality, that

[13]Steiner, *The State of Welfare*.

there is little control of cost, and that it is a very slow and cumbersome process to get day care expanded in areas of high excess demand.

Alternative Modes of Organization and Control of Extrafamily Day Care for Young Children

Private demand for extrafamily day care will grow and will be augmented by public subsidy—perhaps for sound reasons, perhaps for poor ones. Particularly since public policy likely will be an active force behind the expansion, there is the deep obligation to consider carefully how extrafamily day care is to be controlled and organized.

Babysitting arrangements and family day-care homes will, and probably should, continue to provide a good portion of day-care supply. A major policy question is how to facilitate, support, and provide effective overview of noninstitutionalized day care. But the focus here will be on larger, more organized, day-care centers. What are the alternative ways in which demand can be organized? What forms of supply organization should be considered, and how do these link with demand organization? The following discussion will explore how demand and supply are organized under several different institutional regimes.

Evaluation of alternatives, of course, requires that there be some norm. The discussion will not involve explicit analysis of benefits and costs, but will be concerned with rather obvious failings of different regimes. Although gross, the schema seems capable of generating some insight into problems that might arise under different organizational alternatives.[14]

Day-Care Cooperatives / To many, the idea of providing day care through cooperation is attractive. As individual families become increasingly specialized and hence less able or less willing to provide care for their own children, communities

---

[14]In effect, the framework is a generalization of the "anatomy of market failure" approach.

might work out cooperative arrangements without formal organization. In effect, individual demanders of day care would get together and agree to share the "outside" work and the supply of babysitting, with, e.g., five families each agreeing to "sit" once a week.

There are two major difficulties with this kind of arrangement: one is the requirement for jobs with arrangeable hours, and the other is the instability and unreliability of informal arrangements. While there may be volunteers, mothers who "pay" for the care given their children by giving some of their own time to the center, and even a number of pure co-ops, experience with this approach suggests that it is viable for only small segments of society. To provide reliable day care for a large proportion of families, someone must be paid.

Distrust of Private Enterprise and the Market / There appears to be near consensus among those discussing day care that private for-profit enterprise and the "market" represent an unsatisfactory way of organizing the activity. This belief seems to be held by many business leaders as well as by day-care officials. [15] This may appear strange in a country where private enterprise solutions tend to be exalted. What lies behind the apparent rejection?

Unregulated private enterprise—the market—performs the evaluation function by individual consumers deciding what and what not to buy. The supply adjustment is performed by firms seeking profit. An obvious problem with this regime, in its pure form, is that it does not take into account the public interest in quality child care. Many Americans believe that children of disadvantaged families ought to have better care than that which their parents will choose or can afford to purchase, and they are willing to back up their beliefs with money. It would be simple enough, however, to supplement private enterprise with subsidies if externalities were the only complication.

[15]See F. Rudderman, *Child Care and Working Mothers* (Washington, D.C.: Child Welfare League of America, 1958). In particular, see Table 12, p. 78.

However, there is a more basic objection to private enterprise. Although not spelled out explicitly, there apparently is a widespread feeling that private enterprise is not to be trusted, that the control exercised by consumer choice is not likely to be sharp-eyed or well informed about what is best for the children, and that the social responsibility in this matter requires better control.[16]

According to traditional economic theory, consumers are assumed to be experts in knowing what they like, e.g., sweet, juicy oranges, and the alternative goods and services are assumed to be displayed in a way that quality characteristics are evident as well as price. But what if the consumer is not expert or the goods not effectively displayed? Even for oranges, the consumer has little information as to whether they were picked early or late (which may affect their sweetness), or the extent to which color is influenced by dyes rather than sunlight, etc. One can argue here that the costs of uninformed choice are not likely to be serious, and that consumer choice plus governmental regulation which precludes certain producer practices is better than any other evaluative mechanism. One cannot be so sanguine when considering services like child care. Here, the costs of uninformed choice may be very serious. Furthermore, day care is normally provided when the parents are not present, and there is a severe problem of reliable display. The child cannot be considered qualified to evaluate the service. The possibility of occasional sampling plus reports from the child gives some assurance that truly horrendous care is not the rule. But beyond this, how is the parent to judge? And if a parent cannot judge, how is the competitive market supposed to provide effective control?

Obviously the problem is more severe for some parents than for others. Some parents are quite expert in sizing up a place. In some communities there is considerable exchange of information. But for time-pressed inexperienced parents, in a

[16]The flavor comes through strongly in Rudderman, *Child Care and Working Mothers*.

community of like parents, consumer sovereignty is not likely to be an effective mode of public control.

The problem is compounded if public subsidy is to be provided. The public, like the individual parent, wants value for its money. But if a parent cannot judge quality, there is no assurance that public funds are accomplishing anything. In the absence of careful supervision, monies may go straight from the public fisc into the pocket of the owner of the center without influencing the service provided. Clearly, worries of this sort are reflected in past policies that have been biased against providing subsidized day-care funds to proprietary centers.

One possibility is to supplement consumer sovereignty with various modes of quality and safety regulation, and this has been one approach taken in day care. However, it is recognized widely that the degree of overview that can be provided by regularly staffed agencies tends to be limited by resources, and that formal regulation is vulnerable to political pressures from the industry being regulated.

There appears to be a market-failure problem here of a sort not much discussed in the literature.[17] However, people (including economists) may have different opinions regarding its seriousness. Granting the problem sometimes exists, how many parents are really ineffective watchdogs over their child's interests? Is it clear that other modes of organization don't have worse problems?

A Lack of Enthusiasm for Public Provision

It is apparent that for some participants of the day-care debate, the key issue is whether access to good day care ought to be made a "right," with day care (like public schools) financed through taxes rather than prices. It seems highly unlikely,

[17]An important early exception is Arrow, "Uncertainty and the Economics of Medical Care," which points out that in medical care the problem is supposed to be resolved by the professional ethics of the doctor who is not supposed to "maximize his profits." Arrow also points out that most hospitals are "not-for-profit." We shall return to this point later.

however, that public support for this position is so great that
"free" day care will be made available in the foreseeable future for all children. The range and magnitude of subsidy may
increase. But it is likely that a good fraction of day care will
continue to be financed in whole or in part by fees. In any case,
this is not the issue on which I want to focus here; rather, I am
concerned with the way in which the supply of day care is to be
organized, and choice and control exercised.

There is no inherent reason why public agencies should not
provide goods and services to private individuals on a fee-for-
service basis, supplemented by subsidy where appropriate.
However, traditionally, public provision has been associated
with severe restriction on consumer choice. If the public school
system be the model, individual families would face a very
limited choice among day-care centers. Their influence would
have to be made felt, if at all, through "voice" rather than
"exit," to use Hirschman's terms.[18] While a private-enterprise
regime may place too much weight on the judgments of individual families, a regime of public provision tends to place too
little weight on their judgments, and to restrict choice unduly,
if experience with the public school system is a guide.

As has been proposed for public schools, providing families
with a range of choice among institutions can lend more consumer weight to the evaluation machinery. However, as
Downs has pointed out (in the case of school reform),[19] the
traditional public sector supply adjustment machinery must be
modified for increased consumer choice to be effective. In
order for consumer "exit" to have influence, center directors
must have some motivation to attract more children and the
freedom to vary programs so as to make their centers more
attractive. Resources must flow to them in accordance with
their ability to attract customers; if they lose customers their
resources must be cut back. The reward structure, decen-

[18]A. O. Hirschman, *Exit, Voice, and Loyalty* (Cambridge: Harvard University Press, 1970).
[19]A. Downs, "Competition and Community Schools," in *Urban Problems
and Prospects* (Chicago: Markham Press, 1970).

tralized mode of authority, and budget machinery that are required are quite foreign to the public sector as we now know it. No one has yet come up with an attractive proposal for making such a system work.

Public Subsidy to Private Not-for-Profit Day-Care Centers / As indicated earlier, the general drift of public policy over the last decade or so has been, on the one hand, to augment private demand for day care by the provision of public subsidy for certain classes of children and, on the other, to support the evolution of private nonprofit organizations as the preferred delivery vehicle for subsidized day care. While this latter regime accounts for only a small fraction of today's extrafamily day care, in many discussions its rapid expansion is held forth as a target.

Such a regime is compatible with a wide range of mechanisms for organizing demand. Particularly if a considerable degree of consumer freedom of choice can be preserved, there are a number of attractions, at least on the surface, of the not-for-profit as the preferred mode of supply. The objectives of a not-for-profit organization can be defined in terms of the welfare of children and the provision of some particular kind of service, rather than in terms of profit. Within the constraints of financial viability, parents and other interested and expert parties can be given direct access to the processes that determine what is actually being done. Such a regime can, in principle, mitigate some of the more serious problems of lack of parental expertise or interest that make many people nervous about for-profit suppliers, and avoid the monopoly problem latent in a regime of total public provision.

However, unless there is effective overview, the not-for-profit label may be merely a tax dodge, and certainly does not afford much protection from gouging and poor care. While critics of a free-enterprise solution certainly are right in their suspicions of textbook economic arguments, surely many of these in arguing for not-for-profit centers are confusing a figleaf for a solution. Even were profiteering thereby avoided, there still would remain the problem of control of day-care management and of consumer choice. Perhaps the most important reason for the political success of the not-for-profits is that day-care professionals apparently prefer them, because they are a form that professionals are likely to be able to control. Despite its potential advantages as a way for blending professional overview and consumer sovereignty, as discussed above, the not-for-profit system has not allowed much influence to consumers; rather, children are often assigned to individual centers, the actual operation of which is pretty much under the control of day-care management.[20]

Still another difficulty with a regime of nonprofits is that it is neither fish nor fowl with respect to procedures for allocating and reallocating resources. In the absence of an overarching governmental hierarchy, there is no built-in administrative machinery for allocating resources among centers in order to accommodate changing patterns of demand, nor is there the automatic resource allocation associated with for-profit organizations.

Elements of a Viable System

The organization problem for extrafamily day care is quite complex, and certainly will not be solved adequately by being shoved into one or another of our preconceived intellectual bottles. I shall sketch out here what seem to me the elements of a viable system:[21]

I already have committed myself to a system of mixed private and public financing and to some sort of mechanism of control on the demand side that involves a supplementation of consumer sovereignty. How might such a system be designed? One component of such a system certainly should be a mechanism to enable parental judgments to be relatively well informed about alternative day-care centers. This can be

[20]See particularly the chapter by Emma Jackson in Young and Nelson, *Public Policy for Day Care.*
[21]See Young and Nelson, *Public Policy for Day Care.*

achieved in a variety of ways. One possibility would be to require the directors to write up the characteristics of their organization and services, and have these summaries available at a local day-care information and regulatory center, which would be responsible for verifying the claims. This procedure is integral to some of the proposed voucher schemes for elementary education. It is entirely possible to augment official inspection with more informal community inspection procedures.[22]

It is unlikely that such a simple patch-up will be sufficient. A more radical proposal is this. Parents and other interested parties should be able to observe centers in operation at times of their own choosing; each day-care center must operate, as it were, in a fish bowl. Such a requirement would not be viewed kindly by day-care management, whether that management be civil servants or private operators. However, licensing and subsidy regulations can make such operation mandatory. A key function of local regulation could be to check to see that these conditions of openness are being met; in effect, regulation would proceed in large part by seeing that parents and citizens are in a position to regulate.

Open operation can serve two ends. It can enable better-informed choices by parents among centers, thus supplementing the "information-posting" requirement discussed above. But, more important, it can enable parental and citizen overview of the operations of a center. It can facilitate the raising of a well-informed and relatively powerful consumer voice. For where quality is hard to judge, and where learning takes time and effort, control by means of exit or threat of exit is costly and likely to be ineffective. The various studies of day-care centers cited above, and the exposés of institutions delivering services with similar kinds of attributes, like nursing homes, suggest strongly that we must begin to think of nonconventional mechanisms for consumer and citizen overview. The "open institutions" proposal is put forth in that spirit.

Despite Hirschman's warning that a little exit can reduce

[22]Young and Nelson, *Public Policy for Day Care.*

the power of voice, it seems important to keep the possibility of consumer choice and exit as one of the instruments of control. Perhaps the most important reason for having a range of choices is that needs and tastes differ. Control through collective decisions by a group with diverse preferences involves the many difficulties inherent in the theory of public goods. If individual judgments are well informed, the ability of demanders to sort themselves out by picking their own suppliers contributes enormously to the effective operation of the system. There are important implications regarding the nautre of day-care subsidy. If both choice and exit are to be given effective weight, children cannot be assigned to particular centers, nor can their access to subsidy be contingent upon their parents' choice over a very narrow range. Subsidy should in effect take the form of vouchers.[23]

It seems unwise to put too much weight on formal regulatory machinery, and the kinds of monitoring mechanisms discussed above reduce the requirements for formal regulation. Formal regulatory authorities cannot spend much time overseeing particular centers, and thus cannot substitute for continuous consumer or citizen overview. Formal authority generally is forced to use formal standards rather than personal judgments in regulating. Parents may judge that the center provides inferior services and may try to change policies. Or they may withdraw their children. The center may try to persuade them otherwise, but the parents' acts clearly are legitimate. It is something else when an arm of government withdraws a license. Here, due process requires more than the personal judgment of an inspector. Some specific code must be violated. Perhaps the most important role of regulation, under the proposed regime, is to protect and enforce "open" operation.

The requirements for information, openness, and a range of consumer choice, define much of what is needed in organiza-

---

[23]If one insisted upon racial integration, or certain other kinds of groupings of children, as a goal or constraint, then the issue becomes more complicated.

tions that supply day care. So long as these conditions are met there seems no objection to public provision of at least a portion of day-care services, although traditional public provision does not seem to arise under these constraints. There are no innate objections to private, for-profit enterprise that operates according to these ground rules. However, private enterprise of this sort does not look like the textbook model.

Under circumstances where trust and openness, plus some freedom of consumer choice, are important, there is some evidence that private, not-for-profit organizations tend to spring up and take a large share of the market. Both Arrow and Klarman have noted this in the case of hospitals.[24] Many private schools are not for profit. While I see no particular reason for public policy to encourage as a matter of principle the evolution of a nonprofit supply system, the kinds of requirements I have discussed will encourage such a development, and I see no reason for discouraging it.

While a system as described above would appear to be capable of monitoring day-care quality, there is a built-in weakness in the mechanisms that reallocate resources under a nonprofit regime. When demand for the services of a nonprofit center expands, what mechanisms induce its expansion? If it does not expand, what induces new entry at an appropriate location? While a regime of nonprofits with total revenue keyed to the number of children avoids much of the downward inflexibility associated with provision by a public bureaucracy, one would suspect sluggishness in expansion to meet new or expanded needs. Interviews with center directors and people responsible for overall day-care organization in Washington, D.C., reinforce these suspicions.[25] Center directors seem prone to meet excess demand by enlarging the waiting list rather than by enlarging the facility. Establishment of new

[24]Arrow, "Uncertainty and the Economics of Medical Care" and H. Klarman, *The Economics of Health* (New York: Columbia University Press, 1964), particularly Chapter 5.

[25]See the chapter by Jackson in Young and Nelson, *Public Policy for Day Care.*

centers in areas of excess demand appears to depend on the hard work of public-spirited citizens.

A regime of nonprofit institutions thus needs to be complemented by some kind of an overall planning body that is responsible for assessing day-care needs, and has some power to allocate day-care funds, particularly for the establishment of new centers. In what neighborhoods are there large unmet demands for day care? What hours do parents want day care? What components of day care do they consider most important and what are they willing to pay? Obtaining reasonable answers to these questions would be useful even were day care to be provided largely through unregulated private enterprise. Having some group responsible for getting answers to those questions, and with some significant influence on the allocation of funds, is essential in a regime of nonprofits.

The requirement for some kind of an overall planning body seems inherent in the other constraints placed on the solution, which preclude both public provision and private enterprise of the traditional sort. We currently are feeling the pains of not having faced, and certainly not having solved, this problem with respect to hospital investment. If we move toward something like a voucher system in the field of public education, we shall have to develop more effective planning machinery there.

Conclusion

This chapter has been concerned explicitly with extrafamily day care for young children, partly because it is of current policy importance and partly because most discussions of the issues either have ignored or have taken a highly oversimplified view of the economic organization questions involved. But along the way I have alluded to sectors that have characteristics quite similar to those of day care, at least in some of the following respects: there are both private and public interests in the good or service involved; and the good or service is divisible; effective evaluation of the alternatives requires that consumer sovereignty be assisted in various ways; both exit and voice are important control devices. Indeed, it is striking to note that a significant fraction of the articulated dissatisfaction with the microperformance of the American economy involves sectors of this kind. The proposals for open operation and for an overall planning unit seem worthwhile exploring in a large number of these sectors.

7

SUPPORT AND CONTROL OF
THE CREATION OF NEW
TECHNOLOGY: LESSONS
FROM THE SUPERSONIC
TRANSPORT AND THE
BREEDER REACTOR
PROGRAMS

T HE POLICY problem considered in the preceding chapter—day care for young children—was spawned by long-run pervasive changes in the economy which eroded the efficacy of family provision as virtually the sole available organizational form for child care. There are many subtle and complex constraints and desiderata that must be considered in the search for a new organization solution. However, it scarcely seems sensible to worry very much about the ability of a day-care system to generate and absorb radically new knowledge and techniques regarding child care. Clearly we know far less than we would like about how children develop and learn, and, hence, about the best methods of caring for children. It seems desirable that the relevant scientific community have contact with the evolving organization of day care, both as researchers and as experts with some role to play in the governance of the sector. It is unlikely, however, that advances in the understanding of child development can or will proceed so rapidly that the day-care system must strain to stay up with changes in knowledge and practice.

In other sectors of the political economy, advances in understanding and technique play an extremely important, even a dominating, role. The question of who should support and guide the generation of new technological alternatives, and who should screen and select which alternatives will be used, is a central one in these sectors. By and large, economists have not seen that these tasks require any special organizational machinery that goes beyond the market. Scientists and technologists have known in their bones that this was wrong, and that those sectors where we have experienced in the twentieth century the most rapid technological advance have received special assistance from government in the form of money and of organization structure. This is so, for example, for agriculture, medicine, aviation, and atomic energy; the latter two will be a central focus in this chapter.

The last decade has seen a fumbling toward a national technology policy that embraces the economist's appreciation of the fact that R & D machinery cannot proceed independently of other aspects of sectoral governance, and the technologist's appreciation that such machinery must have some room for independent maneuver and some source of independent funds. Sometimes the conservative bias of the economist has been dominant, occasionally the more activist hand of the technologist. We shall be concerned here with the supersonic transport (SST) program of the 1960s, and the liquid metal fast breeder reactor (LMFBR) program of the Atomic Energy Commission during the same period—both of which are instances of the latter case.

These programs, and the nature of the policy debate regarding them, are important for two reasons. First, the particular approach taken by the programs—public subsidy to hasten the development of particular products that are to be produced and sold on competitive markets by private companies—raises some serious questions about efficient strategies for R & D and, more generally, about effective joint governance of R & D and production. Yet, as in the case of day care, the policy dialogue did not fasten on the issue of governance, but rather proceeded (with a few exceptions) to analyze the issue as an investment decision. Thus many of the relevant issues never got posed explicitly. It is not just that the particular proposals were not cost effective; the form of the proposed subsidy was generally an unwise form.

The SST program ultimately was defeated, or at least scotched, but on the basis of argument that did not face squarely the general issues involved; particularly in view of the existence of the Concorde, there continues to be great pressure for government subsidy for R & D on new commercial aircraft.[1] The breeder reactor programs of the AEC (now the Energy Research and Development Administration) have proceeded with only a few murmurs regarding the strategy and rationale of the 1960s. With the energy crunch of the early 1970s, the nation's energy R & D programs have adopted both a broadened strategy and a more adequate rationale, but this has gone largely unnoticed outside the ranks of the professional energy R & D watchers. There is good reason to believe that, in the future, we shall see a growing flow of proposals for federal R & D programs modeled on the two cases considered in this chapter. They are proposals which naturally appeal to technologists.

Second, a disturbing aspect of these two cases is that the pre-SST and pre-LMFBR programs might well serve as appropriate models for the kind of subsidy of, and organizational independence for, R & D that should be adopted in a significantly broadened arena of our political economy. The two cases under study suggest that appropriate government policy in R & D support may be inherently unstable. Therefore, understanding of the forces that generated the programs in question would seem particularly important.

The New Departure: Federal Subsidy for Development of New Products for Production Sale by Private Industry to the General Public

While economists tend to argue that the market should be the dominant mechanism for governing R & D, in fact the role of public finance of R & D is very considerable. In 1972, of a total R & D spending of roughly $28 billion, approximately $16 billion was federal funds. The purposes of the public R & D programs were numerous and diverse, but for the most part can

---

[1]For a discussion, see G. Eads, "U.S. Government Support for Civilian Technology: Economic Theory versus Political Practice," *Research Policy* 3 (1974).

be placed in two categories.[2] The first is the development of new technology for the public sector. The dominant programs here, of course, are defense related, but the government also undertakes or supports R & D aimed at improving the ability of public agencies to protect the public health, guard against dangerous drugs and medicines, support construction of public facilities like airports and roads, enhance educational practice, deter crime, and so forth. In all of these cases the government is charged with performing a particular function, and the R & D is undertaken to permit it to perform more efficiently. But not all publicly funded R & D is directed towards public-sector wants. A good portion is aimed at advancing basic knowledge, or applied knowledge of widespread interest and use or which supports particular important technologies but is not directly tied to particular marketed products. Here, the National Science Foundation (NSF) is the prime example of basic science support and the National Institutes of Health (NIH) perhaps the most clear-cut example of a government agency in support of research underlying a broad technology (medicine). Another important example is long-standing public subsidy of agricultural research done at federal and state experimentation stations. In the early 1960s NASA was a dramatic new departure in government sponsorship of scientific and technological research both for the intrinsic interest of the adventure and because of the belief that diffuse and widespread benefits would be an important by-product.

Governmental spending for both of these purposes has traditions that go back far in American history. The constitutional responsibility for setting and maintaining standards for weights and measures soon led to a small research effort in the Treasury Department. The army arsenals performed R & D on a variety of weapons. Governmental support of research relevant to agriculture goes back well before the Civil War.

[2]For a more detailed discussion, see R. R. Nelson, M. J. Peck, and E. D. Kalachek, *Technology, Economic Growth, and Public Policy* (Washington, D.C.: Brookings Institution, 1967), Chapter 8.

But, as the examples indicate, while the federal government often has supported R & D relevant to private sector
activity, by and large it has steered shy of supporting or under-
taking R & D on a particular product or service whose normal
channel of distribution would be through the market. (There
are exceptions—for example, public funds have developed certain new seed varieties and pharmaceuticals, which then were
produced and sold by private firms.) Rather, governmental R &
D support has aimed to lay the basis for subsequent private
development efforts, not to pre-empt those efforts.

The pre-1960s public support of research related to civil
aviation fits this pattern almost exactly. In 1915 the National
Advisory Committee on Aeronautics (NACA) was created to
spur the development of American aviation. In its heyday,
during the 1920s and 1930s, NACA pioneered in the development and operation of R & D facilities for general use (wind
tunnels, for example) and information collection and dissemination. It supported the development of relevant theory, and it
undertook research on aircraft streamlining, design of engine
parts, properties of fuels, and structural aspects of aircraft
design. It built and tested a variety of experimental hardware.
But NACA did not directly support or direct the development
of particular commercial aircraft. Indeed, the idea that such a
role would be assumed by the federal government was explicitly rejected in the late 1940s when Congress refused to
approve bills that would have appropriated federal funds to
finance the construction of a jet transport prototype.[3]

Until the early 1960s the programs of the AEC in support of
civilian power reactors were similar in spirit to NACA support
of aircraft technology.[4] The amended Atomic Energy Commission Act of 1954 established a more or less explicit division of
responsibility between the AEC and private enterprise, with
government's role limited to supportive research, the building

---

[3]E.g., see the editorial "Costs and Jets," *American Aviation* (June 1, 1948),
1; and "U.S. Airlines to Buy British?," *Aviation Week* (August 29, 1949), 31, 32.

[4]For a discussion, see P. Mullenback, *Civilian Nuclear Power: Economic
Issues and Policy Formation* (New York: Twentieth Century Fund, 1963).

of experimental reactors, the operation of facilities for testing, information dissemination, and so on. Private enterprise clearly was left the job of choosing and financing particular technologies.

During the late 1950s and throughout the 1960s the AEC gradually increased the extent of its involvement in the development of civilian nuclear power, both in terms of subsidy and of detailed planning. By the mid-1960s the AEC was committed to a schedule of bringing to operational level a particular breeder reactor design—the LMFBR. Similarly, during this period the federal program in support of aircraft technology evolved from a traditional NACA type of effort to one of planning and financing the design and development of a particular aircraft, a supersonic transport. These represented major new departures in the government's role in R & D in these areas. It is important to assess the factors that triggered these new departures.

In the breeder reactor case, according to Philip Mullenback,[5] the equipment suppliers cannot be counted among the early enthusiasts for the growing federal push for atomic reactors, much less for the commitment to the LMFBR. Neither can the utilities; indeed, the private utilities tended to resist the building of governmental reactors on a sizeable scale, fearing that this might strengthen the tendency for nuclear power to go public. While there was less resistance on the part of the utilities to government subsidy of private construction and ownership of large experimental plants, in the early days the spirit seems to have been "if you insist that we build, you will have to share the costs," not a spirit of active advocacy. Of course, as the equipment suppliers gradually have invested in their nuclear design and production capabilities, they have grown increasingly enthusiastic about governmental programs that subsidize the procurement of nuclear power. But there was, and is, skepticism within all aspects of the electrical power industry regarding the commitment to the LMFBR.

[5]Ibid.

The early thrust appears to have come largely from within the AEC and the Joint Committee on Atomic Energy. The major speeches advocating the LMFBR during the late 1950s and 1960s were by commissioners and congressmen; these were the active forces behind the gradual escalation of subsidy from assisting studies of the technology (in the mid-1950s) to paying a share of the capital costs and subsidizing reactor design costs (1960) to the present commitment of the AEC to the building and monitoring of the full panoply of equipment needed for a commercial LMFBR.

Similarly, the SST program seems to have been more the result of pushing from within the government than pressure from outside.[6] The program appears to have bubbled up as a result of a coalition between NACA (by then NASA) people who had been researching aspects of supersonic flight in the traditional NACA context, and people at the Federal Aviation Administration (FAA). The early attitude of the airlines appears to have been that an SST was inevitable, but their support for governmental subsidy of development was, at best, guarded. The manufacturers, naturally, were willing to proceed with the development of an SST under governmental funds, but the idea does not seem to have been theirs. In the early stages of the SST program it was not argued that federal funding would play the dominant role, but rather that such funding would have leverage on private funds. As with atomic energy, as the 1960s progressed the extent of governmental subsidy escalated. The key events seems to have been the demise of the B-70, the British-French agreement to proceed with the Concorde, and the growing awareness on the part of SST advocates that the manufacturers would not proceed unless the subsidy was increased substantially. The governmental commitment grew from a $12 million feasibility study in 1961, to (in the early 1960s) cost sharing of up to 50 percent of development cost through prototypes, to (in the late 1960s) 90 percent cost cover-

[6]For a good review, see "Federal Steps to Date in SST Development," *Congressional Digest* (December 1970), 292, 293.

age by the government—and finally, just before the program's demise to an implicit commitment to carry the development through the post-prototype stages.

The Inadequacy of the Arguments, and the Danger of the Strategy

There is no rationale for federal support of R & D that sharply delineates the scope of federal action—that enables clear-cut articulation not only of why it is appropriate to undertake certain programs, but also why other programs should not be undertaken. While at first glance the case for federal defense R & D spending appears to rest simply on the federal responsibility for national security, it becomes apparent that a more subtle argument is required when one asks why federal procurement would not provide adequate incentive for private R & D. The federal government is the world's biggest purchaser of typewriters, but does no R & D on them. The extent to which public R & D backs up public procurement differs greatly from area to area in ways that are not easy to rationalize. The issue of public R & D support in sectors where the goods and services are produced and procured largely by private parties is even muddier. Such support has been rationalized by the argument that R & D has general externalities, or the argument that certain sectors (like agriculture) are structurally unsuited for private R & D; and in some cases a "national interest" in the product of the industry or in the industry itself has been articulated. The aviation and atomic energy cases have involved all of these rationales. But the question always can be raised, why subsidies for one kind of R & D or for a certain industry but not for others?

In the aviation and nuclear power areas the division of responsibility for funding and for governance was significantly better articulated than in other areas, prior to the SST and LMFBR departures. Public funds and a relatively separable R & D governance were provided to support expansion of the knowledge base for technological advance, to support and guide the exploration and testing of new technological regimes, to facilitate flow of knowledge to the producer, and so forth. The producers, feeling the market and assessing the value of new and old technologies, were to make the ultimate decision for development of particular designs. While final product development tends to be the most expensive part of the R & D process, it also is the area where returns are most appropriable, and where market judgment is most appropriate.

The SST and LMFBR programs stemmed in effect, from the discontent of the technologists (whose focus was on the creation of new options) with this division of labor and responsibility. The technologists looked ahead and saw that certain technologies would, in all likelihood, play a significant economic role in the future. These technologies were, in a sense, inevitable. Yet the private companies who had legitimate responsibility to make development commitments to particular technologies were not moving rapidly on these new options. The response of the technologists was to argue for governmental funds to do what they thought private firms ought to be doing but were not.

It was not argued that the technologies in these sectors were stagnating under the existing regime, or that some urgent national goal compelled acceleration. In aviation, technological progress had been extremely rapid, successive generations of new aircraft had made travel vastly faster and more comfortable, and prices of air travel (even not counting the great improvements in quality) had fallen relative to average prices. Indeed, at least one recent study concluded that the development of new aircraft perhaps has proceeded at too fast a rate, with CAB rate control authority precluding effective price competition by older planes to counter the speed advantages of the new craft, and thus providing an artificially profitable market for new high-performance aircraft.[7]

[7]W. A. Jordon, *Airline Regulation in America: Effects and Imperfections* (Baltimore: Johns Hopkins University Press, 1971), especially Chapter 3, "Rivalry Through Service Quality."

In view of the current alarm about energy, it is difficult to think back a decade. But at the time the LMFBR program began to take shape, there was no perception of crisis, or even of impending hard times regarding the price and availability of conventional fuel, which might make early achievement of a breeder a high-return social policy. Fuel prices had been falling, not rising, in large part because the long-run rate of productivity growth in the production of electric power was more than three times the national average. In their monumental study published in 1960 and available at the time of the LMFBR decision, Schurr and Netchert projected that coal reserves were ample to meet the demands at least to the end of the century without rising costs. They thought petroleum reserves were more problematical, but for the purposes of generation of electricity, they argued that coal could be substituted for petroleum without difficulty.[8] The 1965 study *Energy R and D and National Progress,* which was undertaken with the express purpose of identifying sources of concern, reached the conclusion that significant shortages of conventional fuels, or sharply rising costs of extraction, were not likely in this century.[9] With the wonderful vision of hindsight we now can see that these studies were overly optimistic. However, the advocates of the LMFBR crash program did not know then what we know now, nor did they argue effectively against the forecasts available at that time.

What, then, were the arguments for the programs? The first line of argument was that large financial requirements and a long lead time, combined with uncertainty about returns and cost, might be deterring private firms from taking actions with a high expected rate of return. This position could not stand scrutiny for two reasons. First, in a number of cases private firms had raised funds on their own that were comparable to those involved in the projects under consideration here. For

[8] S. Schurr and B. Netchert, *Energy in the American Economy* (Baltimore: Johns Hopkins University Press, 1960).

[9] *Energy R and D and National Progress* (Washington, D.C.: U.S. Government Printing Office, 1965).

example, IBM is reported to have risked $5 billion in the early
1960s to develop the System 360 family of computers.[10] Second, and more important, the expected rates of return on the
projects were not high. Even cost-benefit studies done by
program advocates showed a rate of return for the SST, and for
the LMFBR, that was low compared with typical private investment projects, under what many outsiders regarded as
rigged assumptions.[11] That the expected rate of return was
quite low was known to those who argued for the program on
grounds of large capital expense requirements. Had this not
been believed both in government and in industry, much more
consideration would have been given to governmental loans
and risk sharing, rather than one form or another of subsidy.

The second line of argument was that, in these cases, the
social rate of return exceeded the private rate. However, as
suggested above, a case for some spillover benefit can be made
for virtually any technology and for almost any R & D project.
The case for having public funds concentrated on basic and
exploratory R & D is that these have a larger share of externalities than does final product development. What then were
the "strong externalities" arguments for putting public funds
into final product development in these two cases?

Essentially the argument was that it is better for society to
have a good thing earlier rather than later. In the cases of both
atomic energy and the supersonic transport, it was apparent
that the technologies would be valuable to have around, if they
achieved anything close to their potential, and if their environmental problems could be resolved. In the cost-benefit studies
of the breeder reactor program, a considerable amount was

[10]T. A. Wise, "IBM's $5,000,000,000 Gamble," *Fortune* (September
1966), 118

[11]For a review and critique of these studies, see L. Merewitz and S. H.
Sosnick, *The Budget's New Clothes: A Critique of Planning-Programming-
Budgeting and Benefit-Cost Analysis* (Chicago: Markham Publishing Co.,
1971). See also "Report of SST Ad Hoc Review Committee, Economic Sub-
committee," reprinted in House Appropriations Committee, *Hearings: Department of Transportation and Related Agencies Appropriations for 1970* (91st
Congress, 1st Session), pt. 3, "Civil Supersonic Aircraft Development," pp.
321–324.

made of the fact that, given the large and rapidly growing market for electric power, hastening the day that we have breeder reactors that are superior economically to existing technologies would enable us to start our benefit flow earlier, and thus would enhance the total benefits we would reap. In the SST studies, the same kind of argument was employed, and a supplementary point argued. It was claimed that failure to exploit the technology embodied in the supersonic transport at the earliest possible moment would mean a loss of technological leadership, which in turn would mean an irreversible loss of world commercial position. The advent of the British-French program to develop the Concorde of course accentuated these arguments.

On reflection these kinds of "externalities" arguments really aren't very persuasive, and certainly don't apply to the proposed programs. In the first place, in these cases (and more generally) it is hard to see a "social benefit" in hastened development that significantly exceeds benefits that would appear to business firms as profit opportunities. Interest rates put a premium on earlier rather than later returns, and often it is argued that private incentives focus too much, not too little, attention on early benefits. If the argument were changed to posit that the private rate of time discount is too high to induce private funding on projects whose payoff will occur only with a long time lag, then the implications would seem to be support of an old-style NACA or AEC policy of funding of experimental work, not a crash program. Nor does the "commercial leadership and export revenue" argument point to social benefits as opposed to private benefits; certainly it does not point to R & D as an instrument for the achievement of such social purposes.

The basic reason why private investment funds were not flowing into an accelerated development program can be ascribed not to "externalities," but rather to the high cost and innate inefficiencies involved in rushing a technology. Common sense, history, and detailed analysis all tell us that there is a time/cost trade-off.[12] Public subsidy can buy us time, but we pay for speed. The costs of hastened development must be weighed against the benefits of gaining an attractive technology sooner. While the cost-benefit studies stressed the benefits of faster achievement, they either ignored or denied that we could achieve the same results more cheaply if we hurried less. But this was really the issue. Why were the costs and risks too great in these programs for private enterprise to bear? In good part because at the targeted rate of development one could not proceed sequentially and in small bites, keeping options alive and committing large funds to any one only when the evidence in its favor was clear.

The organizational model for the LMFBR and SST proposals of course was that of the Manhattan Project to develop the atomic bomb during World War II, Project Apollo, and much of military R & D. The style involves a willingness to make large early bets on particular technological options and force these through, or engage in parallel efforts at very high cost. The strategy can buy rapid technical progress, but only at enormous cost and with enormous waste.

One of the more striking aspects of the history of technological advance in most American industries is the diversity of sources. New products, processes, inputs, and equipment for an industry have come from firms in the industry, suppliers, purchasers, new entrants to the industry, and individual outside inventors. The process certainly has not been orderly or planned, but one has the impression that had one tried to impose order and a central plan the results would have been worse. Many developments that earlier seemed to be very promising did not pan out. Many important breakthroughs were relatively unexpected and were not supported by the experts in the field. While detailed case histories are not plenti-

[12]For a discussion, see F. M. Scherer, "Government Research and Development Programs," in R. Dorfman (ed.), *Measuring the Benefits of Government Expenditures* (Washington, D.C.: Brookings Institution, 1965).

ful, one has the impression that in most of the technically progressive industries, like chemicals and electronics, most of the bad bets were rather quickly abandoned, particularly if someone else was coming up with a better solution, and good new ideas generally had a variety of paths to get their case heard.[13]

Military R & D programs since the mid-50s, the civil reactor programs, and the supersonic transport experience are in sad contrast. In all of these areas the early batting average has been dismal. However, there has been a tendency to stick with the game plan despite mounting evidence that it is not a good one; this tendency appears only in exceptional cases in areas where R & D is more decentralized and competitive. The case of Convair's throwing good money after bad on the 880 development rightly is regarded as an aberration, though the fact that General Dynamics had learned its style in military R & D undoubtedly was a contributing factor. But this kind of thing is the rule, not the exception in military R & D. The B-58 and TFX were pushed all the way through development despite mounting unfavorable evidence. The B-70 and Skybolt were halted short of procurement, but long after signals were clear that they were bad ideas. Advocates of the SST and LMFBR implicitly denied the relevance of this experience. The heart of the programs was early commitment of governmental funds to a particular design.[14] In the case of the supersonic stransport, it is highly unlikely that Boeing would have persisted so long in pushing its swing-wing SST design had the bulk of the funds been its own, and had it the ability to make that decision on its

[13]See, for example, the case studies in J. Jewkes, D. Sawers, and R. Stillerman, *The Sources of Invention* (New York: St. Martin's Press, 1970); M. J. Peck, *Competition in the Aluminum Industry* (Cambridge: Harvard University Press, 1961); R. Miller and D. Sawers, *The Technical Development of Modern Aviation* (London: Routledge and Kegan Paul, 1968), and Nelson, Peck, and Kalachek, *Technology, Economic Growth, and Public Policy.*

[14]See the discussion in B. Klein, A. Marshall, W. Meckling, and F. M. Scherer, *The Rate and Direction of Inventive Activity* (Princeton, N.J.: Princeton University Press, 1962).

own. The result, of course, was a clear technological failure. Similarly, throughout the history of the AEC power reactor program there have been complaints that the AEC was persisting in R & D on a design long after evidence had accumulated that the route was not an attractive one, and also that the AEC has been very sticky about initiating work on new concepts. The LMFBR still is a very risky design, and it does not make much sense to place all of our chips on it. Only the overall expansion of energy R & D budgets in the early 1970s has gotten us off that hook.

The Problem of R & D Governance

While a strong case can be made against these programs viewed as social investment projects, the cost-benefit kind of analysis does not probe deeply enough. Perhaps the most basic reason why the two programs under consideration were unwise is that they failed to come to grips with the fact that R & D governance, and the governance of the provision of the goods and services with which R & D is connected, need close integration at the level of product or process development. The case for some autonomy of R & D governance is persuasive at the level of exploratory R & D—the kind of work NACA and the AEC used to stress. But autonomy at the product development level is foolish or downright dangerous.

To establish relative autonomy of product development decision in a sector where new products must meet a relatively rigorous market test is to court commercial disaster. That the United States has dominated the commercial aircraft market in the postwar period is undeniable. Recent estimates reveal that over 80 percent of the world's commercial airline fleet was built in this country. Phillips's research makes it clear, however, that this dominant commercial position rests not only on the general technical virtuosity of U.S.-built commercial aircraft but also on the good record of American manufacturers in deciding when to embody technological advances in commercial products.[15] This record undoubtedly has beed aided by the fact that in each case, the decision to produce a commercial design has been made by a private company risking its own funds. There is no doubt, for example, that if Congress had been willing to appropriate the necessary funds in 1948, the United States and not Britain could have been the first to introduce jet transports into commercial service. It is clear from a study of the designs then being proposed, however, that the early U.S. jet transports would have been no more viable commercially than were the Comet I and Comet II. And how much would it have aided the reputation of the American commercial aircraft industry had it, and not the British, been the one to discover the catastrophic effects on pressurized aircraft of metal fatigue?

In contrast to the U.S. experience, the record of the British aircraft industry in the postwar period has been dismal. The British government has been prepared to cover up to 50 percent of the costs of launching civil aircraft designs and to assure a base market for these designs by requiring British flag carriers to purchase the resulting product, regardless of operating costs.[16] As a result the British have rung up a string of techno-

[15]A. Phillips, *Technological Change and the Market for Commercial Aircraft* (Lexington, Mass.: D.C. Heath & Co., 1973). This point is also stressed by Miller and Sawers, *Modern Aviation*, which points out, for example, that the Comet I, with operating costs almost three times as great as the DC-6B, could make money only as long as only one carrier on a route was operating it. As soon as a second carrier offered Comet service, the first carrier's load factor would drop far below break-even level. This factor obviously limited the market for the Comet in spite of its substantial advantage in speed over piston aircraft.

[16]R. E. Baldwin, *Nontariff Distortions of International Trade* (Washington, D.C.: Brookings Institution, 1970). This latter commitment alone was costing the British government an estimated $80 million in subsidy to British European Airways in 1968.

Miller and Sawers, *Modern Aviation*, lists the total direct contributions (prototype and production support) by the British government for commercial aircraft jet engines and airframes between 1945 and 1965 (including the VC-10, Trident, and BAC-111 but excluding the Concorde) as 61 million pounds and 67 million pounds respectively. Total repayment to that time amounted to 13 million and 12 million pounds. No engine (of seven) and only one aircraft (of ten) had produced royalty payments to the government in excess of the

logical successes that, by and large, have been commercial failures. Even the massive infusion of government aid has not served to maintain the health of the British aircraft industry, and, with few exceptions, the aircraft have generated nowhere near the hoped-for volume of export earnings.

When there is no powerful autonomous value-setting mechanism, like a market or a public agency not strongly influenced by producer interests, the problems are even more serious. It is disturbing that there was not more vocal concern about the implications of a governmental stake in the supersonic transport, particularly given the explicit revenue-sharing provisions of the program in its later stages. Even without a financial stake, the government agencies, and the higher executives and members of Congress who support a program, have a personal credibility stake in the success of the products and processes they push. It was relatively clear that the success of the SST program, measured along almost any dimension that had been talked about, would have depended highly on the fare structure allowed and encouraged by the CAB. The CAB could have gone a long way toward making the SST program a financial success by fighting for high fares (to cover the higher costs of the SST relative to the jumbo jets) and uniform fares (so that the lower-cost technology would not be able to compete in the dimension where it was strongest).

It is rather surprising that the producers of coal and oil, and of power-generating equipment using conventional fuels, have not raised more noise than they have about the pressure being applied to the utilities by the AEC to install nuclear rather than conventional power. While the evidence on the nature of thermopollution and nuclear waste problems if far from clear, and it well may be that nuclear power still looks good compared to conventional power in terms of pollution and waste, we all should feel some discomfort that a strong governmental lobby has a stake in the issue. I do not want the reader to carry away

government's contribution toward the development, even not allowing for interest.

the impression that the central problem of R & D policy is to contain the aggressive technologists. In many cases this is a problem. But at least as important is somehow to enhance the pace of advance of scientific understanding and technology regarding the large share of human activity where progress has been lamentably small. Here the conservatism of the economist, who tends to see little need for autonomous R & D unshackled from the short-run incentives affecting both business firm and government bureaucracy, is at least as much a danger as the often naive optimism of the R & D buff.

The disparities in rates of growth of productivity across our economic sectors have been enormous. To cite illustrative numbers, the percentage yearly increase in output per worker for the period 1948–1966 was 5.6 in farming, 4.6 in mining, 2.9 in manufacturing; in contrast, the figure for construction was 2.0 percent, for general services, 1.2 percent.[17] These broad sectoral categories themselves conceal great disparities. Within the manufacturing sector, productivity growth in chemicals was 6.0 percent a year, in petroleum refining 5.5 percent, in electrical equipment 4.1 percent, while down at the other end of the spectrum, productivity growth in apparel was 2.2 percent a year, in leather products 1.7 percent. By and large (and with a number of important exceptions) those industries that produced products or that employed products in an essential way in the delivery of services (like airlines) experienced productivity growth at a significantly faster rate than those sectors delivering personal services.

The consequences of this great imbalance in rates of technological progress across different sectors and activities have been profound. Empirical evidence strongly confirms the prediction of economic theory that prices of different industries should move with total factor productivity. The consequences of sharply differing rates of productivity growth have been significant changes in our relative price (and cost) structure.

[17]These figures are from J. Kendrick, *Postwar Productivity Trends in the United States,* 1948–1969 (National Bureau of Economic Research, 1974).

Thus we have experienced sharply rising relative costs and, sometimes, deteriorating quality in the slow-productivity-growth industries—housing, personal services, education, and a whole collection of government-provided services like garbage collection and street cleaning. Many of the complaints that people have about the way the American economy has evolved seem related to this unbalanced evolution of technology.

Perhaps nothing much can be done about it. But the dramatic success that has been achieved through government-supported programs in several of our key sectors suggests that we might want to give it a try. Much more attention ought to be given to our experience in agriculture than has been given up to now. Ironically, there is much to be learned from the old NACA experience and the earlier days of the AEC. In all of these sectors we seemed to have achieved a highly efficacious mix of governance of R & D, with applied R & D being relatively closely linked to the market, and basic research and exploratory development being given a much looser rein, and separate support. It is highly unlikely that the exact form of the organizations adopted in our successful sectors can be carried over to the new areas. Indeed it is not clear even what that would mean, since the structures differ significantly among themselves. But I propose that posing the problem in terms of the design of a semiautonomous structure for certain kinds of R & D is a useful way to begin the search.

The cases discussed in this chapter, however, should warn us of a danger. Separate R & D organization seems to be infected with a camel's nose syndrome. Unless carefully monitored, it becomes a powerful lobbyist of new technology for its own sake. Controlling independent R & D organization may be as difficult as designing it. Certainly both tasks require a sophisticated awareness of the purposes, and the dangers, of R & D autonomy.

8

THE GOVERNANCE OF ECONOMIC ACTIVITY IN A WORLD OF CHANGE

THE CASE STUDIES presented in the preceding two chapters have certain important points in common. In both the case of day care and the case of the SST, much of the policy discussion was focused on particular investment proposals. However, if my diagnosis is accepted, in order to analyze the issues effectively in both cases it is necessary to interpret the specific investment proposals as symptomatic of a larger set of questions about the organization and governance of particular activities. And in both cases it is highly useful to set the problem in a historical context.

The interpretation of the problem as "organizational" is important for several reasons. First, the functioning of the organizational structure surrounding the particular investment proposals is a key to determining whether and how the proposals would work out, even on their own terms. Thus, it became apparent, upon probing, that no real structure exists for the effective allocation of day care subsidy. In the SST case, the pre-emption of market judgment at the development level but not at the procurement level seemed foreordained, in the absence of other policies, to lead to a subsidized plane that no one would buy. Second, in both cases, the particular proposals appear, after analysis, to be part of a wider class of complaints about the prevailing organizational structure. Thus, it is apparent that there are a variety of pressures from many sources for an augmented system of extrafamily child care. The SST and LMFBR cases seem to be exemplars of a wide discontent among technologists in those fields with the conservativeness of market judgments. Third, the nature of the organizational alternatives that could meet the legitimate complaints about the prevailing structure is far from obvious. Prefabricated

general-purpose organizational forms will not do the trick.
Some special-purpose designing appears needed.

A historical perspective on the problems serves to set the
organizational analysis in context. In the case of day care, a
historical perspective points the analysis toward the dramatic
changes which have occurred and are occurring in the basic
demographic situation, something hardly mentioned in the
more traditional studies focused on cost-benefit analysis. In the
supersonic and breeder reactor cases, analysis of the genesis of
the policy debate enables one to see the key role of the internal
dynamics of government agencies and programs, and hence to
be wary about the problem of control.

I propose that many other major policy problems of the day
can be interpreted within this basic intellectual frame—as pressures on prevailing organizational structure, stemming from
new circumstances and perceptions, and requiring search for
organizational changes that can cope with the new situations.
Consider, for example, the current malaise regarding education. On the surface are a potpourri of specific proposals that
tend to be analyzed as specific programs. But behind the scenes
is a deeper organizational problem. With productivity rising
much faster in most other sectors than in education and wage
rates rising with average national productivity, educational
costs have risen steeply relative to the average costs of other
economic activities. This in itself would have stirred up a search
for a way to organize the education sector so that it will be better
able to generate new alternatives which can keep costs down.
But in addition we have been asking more of the educational
system than we used to. Among other things, we are demanding that it play a leading role in cracking a deeply rooted and
continuing pattern of discrimination, as well as provide an
excellent education for those who will be going on to post-
secondary education. The disparate and often conflicting arguments about reform of the educational system reflects a search
for a (possibly nonexistent) organizational regime that will meet
new demands and adapt to new cost conditions.

The stress and strain apparent in our present system of medical care also can be interpreted in terms of changes that have severely strained the old regime. Growing general affluence and political pressures to even out inequality of access to certain goods and services by themselves would have increased significantly demand for medical care and required that the "means test" play a diminishing role in determining who got what kind of service. But the problem has been compounded greatly by notions, part realistic and part exaggerated, of what advances in medical knowledge and technology have made possible. People are demanding to be relieved of forms of suffering and death that several years ago were accepted as inevitable. The erosion of our willingness to use ability to pay as a major component of the demand-generating system, combined with the growing complexity of medical knowledge, has increased the role of physician judgment in determining what is done and not done, and blunted the role of "cost" in that decision. In medicine we are searching for a regime of governance that can determine who gets what care in an informed and equitable fashion, without unduly escalating total medical care costs.

Our present environmental problems also clearly are the result both of changes in relative values at the margin, and of changed circumstances. As general affluence has risen, people are willing to trade off more material goods for environmental amenities. At the same time, general economic growth and the particular technological slant it has taken have made environmental amenities both more scarce and more in jeopardy. The key policy problem is somehow to devise a new governing apparatus that will reflect new values and circumstances effectively.

These examples, and the ones treated in more detail in the preceding chapters, obviously differ in many respects. This diversity should warn us against simple-minded general-purpose diagnosis and remedy. But the common aspects of the examples suggest that it may be useful to develop a general appreciation of the problems of governance of economic activity in a world of change.

The Economic Organization Question Revisited

The formal apparatus of contemporary economic theory unfortunately is biased toward setting the analysis of economic organization in a static frame. In virtually every introductory economics textbook, and in almost all advanced mathematical treatises on the topic, resources, technologies, and preferences of citizens have been taken as given. In formal "welfare economics" the economic problem is viewed as that of finding an allocation of resources to different existing technologies for the production of different goods and services so as to maximize consumer welfare, given prevailing preferences. It may not be apparent that this way of posing the economic problem calls for a solution in terms of organization structure. Certainly the static perspective obfuscates many of the underlying organizational issues. However, economists long have recognized that behind the allocation problem is an organizational problem; that the really important decision is the choice of machinery to make the more detailed decisions.

The organizational problem resides in the following: In order to solve the economic allocation problem a vast amount of data are needed—regarding resource availabilities, alternative technologies, tastes—which must be collected from scattered places and somehow processed to solve the allocation problem. The computations involved in finding an optimal solution are staggering, yet somehow these calculations must be undertaken, and the relevant results made available to those with authority over the resource allocation process. Given that considerable division of labor is involved in the production process, a complex action signaling system is needed to assure that the separate economic actors will know what to do to coordinate their actions so as to optimize the system as a whole. Since detailed monitoring of every action from the center is not possible, some kind of an incentive system is required so that the appropriate data, signals, and actions required of the actors in the system will be motivated. Economic allocation is the result of institutional machinery carrying out these functions, well or poorly.

The question of the appropriate form of economic organization has a long and honorable intellectual history in economics, as does advocacy of a free-enterprise solution to that question, although various times and various authors have held different premises and perceptions. The *Wealth of Nations* is, to a large extent, an essay advocating the "freeing up" the prevailing market machinery from various "artificial" constraints.

For the purposes of this essay it is useful to dwell a bit on the more recent argument between Mises and Lange on the virtues of free enterprise and the viability of a socialist alternative.[1] The point made by Mises is that a "market" is an organizational structure that can take care of the data collection-computation-signaling-incentive problem in a parsimonious way, and that no one has provided a plausible blueprint by which these functions can be accomplished in a regime oriented around a central planning agency which abandoned real markets. Lange's response was to propose an organizational structure, consonant with public ownership of capital, that he argued would solve the economic problem. While the verbal debate was not bound by modern formal theory, it was disciplined by formal theory and by its static frame. Throughout the Mises-Lange discussion of the economic organization question, the issue was posed as that of the control of clerks. The organizational problem was seen as that of getting the individual economic actors to be diligent about observing the right things, sending accurate and appropriate information, responding to signals with appropriate actions. This image of the organizational problem is latent in the Langian socialist-organization proposal.

[1]See L. V. Mises, "Economic Calculation in Socialism," and O. Lange, "On the Economic Theory of Socialism," both reprinted in M. Bornstein, *Comparative Economic Systems: Models and Cases* (Homewood, Ill.: Richard D. Irwin, 1969).

There are important exceptions to the static perspective. Hayek's[2] objection to Lange's proposal is based on the point that the conditions facing the economic system—resources, technologies, and preferences—tend to be variable, and thus conditions of economic optimization will change. The variations that Hayek had in mind, particularly variations in demand for goods and availability of certain kinds of resources, he argued, were particular to place and time, and unpredictable. Speedy, well-directed response requires, he suggested, real decentralization of authority and real motivation to attend to the changing particulars. He argued that, these circumstances obtaining, simulated socialist markets were likely to operate much more sluggishly than real capitalist markets. While he did not spell out in any detailed way why this should be the case, obviously he did not believe that bureaucratic decentralization would be effective. It is apparent that many contemporary economists agree with him.

Clearly, speed and accuracy of response to changing demand and factor supply conditions is an important desideratum of economic organization. One of the key issues in the day care policy dialogue is whether nonmarket supply mechanisms can be made flexible and adaptive. While the heterodox literature places considerable stress on the adaptability of a market-organized sector, it is important to recognize that the theoretical underpinnings of this position are weak, and do not rest comfortably on the foundations provided by traditional formal welfare economics. Analysis of adaptability requires explicit attention to dynamic speed of response, and stability, rather than focus on equilibrium conditions alone.

Still other participants in the comparative economic systems debate place even heavier emphasis on the alleged dynamic advantages of market capitalism. The early Schumpeter certainly did not view the economic problem as that of the

[2]F. Hayek, "The Uses of Knowledge in a Society," *American Economic Review*, September 1945.

control of clerks.[3] His belief was that not only preferences and resources, but also technologies, change over time. Schumpeter, and Marx before him, saw the real power of a capitalist market system in terms of the ability of that system to spur innovation. He also believed that competitive markets provided an environment (monitored by final consumers and powered by competition) that controls the processes of technological change and spreads benefits widely. In his later writings, he recanted the proposition that market competition was necessary for the generation of innovation, positing that in large corporate enterprises, innovation itself has become largely routinized. Therefore, he foresaw no particular disadvantages from socialization of the innovation process, as well as the more routine activities of the economy. The SST policy issue, of course, hinges partly on the question of whether innovation can be planned in a highly predictable way. Many contemporary economists still take the early Schumpeterian position that a key advantage of a market system over a centrally planned one is that it provides a better innovation-generating and -selecting structure. But this proposition rests on very different grounds from the traditional welfare economics arguments.

The discussion of comparative economic organization clearly has been plagued by narrowness and intellectual schizophrenia. The narrowness of the economists' conception of organizational alternatives has been a central theme throughout this essay. Too often the issue has been posed as that of planning versus the market, with little serious attention paid to the fact that there are a variety of possible blends of planning and the market, that both planning and the market can take a wide variety of different forms, and that certain forms of organization defy labeling as one, the other, or a blend. There is no point here in repeating the earlier discussion. Suffice it to say that the issues of day-care policy and the SST controversy

[3]J. Schumpeter, *The Theory of Economic Development* (Cambridge: Harvard University Press, 1934).

highlight the difficulty with this kind of simple-minded characterization of alternatives. Reality refuses to mimic art. Mixed
and complex forms dominate the economic system. We must
learn to analyze these in their own terms.

The point I want to stress here is the rather surprising
failure of the treatises that list the standard arguments for
market organization to recognize the contradiction between
those arguments for market structure which are based on the
premise that the behavior of a competitive regime will be
Pareto optimal, and those arguments for real markets which are
focused on the alleged flexibility and responsiveness of such a
regime—or even more in tension, the argument that market
organization provides a splendid evolutionary system. The first
argument views the situation statically, and sees the economic
problem as one of the effective control of clerks. The latter two
arguments view the economic system as in flux, and aim for
adaptive and creative response. The arguments involve quite
different perceptions of the structure of the economic organizational problem.

Obviously I am committed to the latter perspective. This is
not to deny the importance of the "control of clerks" function.
However, I would argue that in a static world this is relatively
easy. The difficult part of economic systems design is to assure
appropriate responsiveness to external change, and creativity
and selection regarding innovation.

Economic Organization as Defining an Adaptive Evolutionary System

A strong case can be made that to look at economic organization as defining an adaptive and evolutionary system, rather
than a maximizing one, far from a radically new appreciation, is
to hark back to the classical economists. Schumpeter is much
closer intellectually to Marshall and Smith than he is to Samuel-
son and Arrow. However, regardless of the sanctity of our
intellectual heritage, it is apparent that an evolutionary per-

spective on economic organization is quite different from that contained in contemporary formal economic theory.

The key premises of such a perspective on the organization problem seem to me to be these.[4] First, resources, preferences, and technologies are not given and fixed; they will change over time. Second, the performance of an economic sector in the long run is dependent, to a considerable degree, upon how the sector responds to changes generated elsewhere in the economic system that are reflected in changes in its own factor-supply and product-demand conditions, and on how it generates new ways of doing things. The processes of adaptation and innovation of course are not independent; effective adaptation often requires appropriate innovation, and innovation often is stimulated by changes in demand and supply conditions. Third, and this is crucial, responses to changed external conditions and innovation cannot be analyzed as if they were "optimizing" processes. Rather, they need to be understood as adaptive and stochastic.

These premises, while quite general, do provide a framework for appreciation of many policy problems. In particular, an explicitly evolutionary perspective suggests a way of looking at the components of organizational structure. The "demand" machinery of the earlier discussion takes the form of a "selection environment" that signals preferences of "consumers" to suppliers and innovators, and that rewards and punishes various actions on the part of the "suppliers." Within a given selection regime, the nature of what is most reinforced or deterred may vary as a result of changing external conditions. Within a selection regime of "consumer purchase," for example, what is purchased may depend on consumer income and on

[4]The formal model behind this articulation is being developed by Sidney Winter and myself, and has been discussed in several places. See particularly R. Nelson, "Issues and Suggestions for the Study of Industrial Organization in a Regime of Rapid Technological Change," in V. Fuchs, ed., *Policy Issues and Research Opportunities in Industrial Organization* (New York: Columbia University Press for the NBER, 1972). Also, R. Nelson and S. Winter, "Growth Theory from an Evolutionary Perspective: The Differential Productivity Puzzle," *American Economic Review,* May 1975.

the price and characteristics of other kinds of goods, as well as on the characteristics of what is offered at what terms by suppliers within the sector under consideration. A governmental "budgetary process" is part of a selection environment for programs proposed by government agencies. But what amount is budgeted for what program may depend on the nature of the programs under way or proposed by other government agencies, overall fiscal tightness, the state of peace or war, recent elections, and so forth.

Many selection environments are quite complex. Consider the selection environment impinging on public schools in a given area. The selection environment involves the locational patterns of families with school-age children, and the families decisions about whether they will send their children to public or private schools. It also includes a political budgetary process, special referendums on school tax and bond issues, and a variety of mechanisms whereby interested parties, parents or politicians, can try to influence the behavior of various public school officials, from superintendents to teachers.

The way "supply" is organized determines the nature of the supply response to the incentives and constraints provided by the selection environment. The analysis roughly corresponds to "survival and expansion of the fittest" in biological theory. In an economic sector, the mechanisms involved are of two roughly separable sorts; the characterization of supply can focus on these dimensions. One dimension of supply response can be described by the rules guiding the expansion or contraction of particular suppliers using particular policies or producing particular goods. The other dimension can be described by the rules by which suppliers shift to different policies, products, or modes of production. In market-supply systems, the supply mechanism is organized around profit and profit incentive, which (modified by the workings of capital markets) provide the resources as well as the stimulus for expansion or pressures for contraction. Profit and profit incentive also influence the composition of products and processes of any supplier. In sectors where supply is governmentally provided, the supply-adjustment mechanism is made up of the legal and financial constraints that have been created by the political budget decision, together with the supplier's desire to design a next-year's budget proposal that will appeal to the higher political authority and enable the agency to do what it wants to do. In a school system, individual schools must live within their budgets, which may in part be keyed to enrollments. Children who show up at a particular school to receive an education are to be admitted. Courses of instruction and modes of teaching are largely determined within the school system itself, subject to the occasional vetoes or mandates of the political machinery and to more or less continuing pressures from parents and other citizens.

The structure that generates innovations (mutations) may be entirely contained by the supply organization—or there may be a separable component. The old NACA was a semi-autonomous source of certain kinds of aircraft R & D. The NIH provide a mechanism for funding and guiding biomedical R & D quite separate from the structure that governs the day-by-day organization of medical care or the routine investment decisions about where hospitals will be located. The technology of many economic sectors rests intellectually on scientific fields that are of interest to university faculty members. Thus, innovation in the electronics industry is linked to the scientific interests of academics whose grant proposals are processed by the NSF.

These three organizational components—demand, supply, and innovation generation—are conceptually separable. However, their interaction is essential to the performance of the sector in question. And the appropriate design of one cannot be specified independently of a detailed understanding of the design of the others. Thus, for example, concern about the efficacy of individual consumer sovereignty as the selection environment for day care raises questions about whether for-profit organizations are the appropriate way to organize supply.

On the other hand, a decision to organize supply along not-for-profit lines, coupled with a decision not to assign parents to day-care centers but rather to let them make their own choice, means that special capital-allocation machinery is needed.

The SST debate also involved the coherence of the organization structure. If it could be argued persuasively that the selection environment for new civilian aircraft should weight heavily such noncommercial values as American prestige or technological leadership per se, then the argument that profit incentives alone could not effectively guide new aircraft design would be persuasive. The problem then would be to establish an effective mechanism for weighing and funding noncommercial values in aircraft procurement. On the other hand, if market values were accepted as legitimate indicators of aircraft values, the case for governmental subsidy of the design of particular aircraft would have to rest on more subtle allegations of market failure in the R & D process. But then it would not make sense to subsidize R & D unless the particular aircraft looked commercially attractive, assuming its design costs could be covered.

I stated above that neither Hayek's argument about the rapid adaptation characteristics of real market systems, nor Schumpeter's arguments about the efficacy of market competition in inducing innovation, can be analyzed within the traditional static model of the economic problem. The framework of analysis I have just sketched does provide a language for discussing these arguments, and the two case studies presented earlier are good ones for making the discussion concrete. It should be apparent that, while I am sympathetic to the way Hayek and Schumpeter posed the economic problem, I believe that their arguments in favor of market solutions are oversimplified. Hayek argued that market organization leads to rapid and effective response to changes in the particular situations of time and place. But it is not at all clear that for-profit market supply invariably leads to producers' response to consumer demands. Recall Henry Ford's remark that Americans can have

any color Ford they desire, so long as it is black, or consider
more current examples: the failure of American automobile
companies to recognize and respond quickly to the rising demands for small cars during the 1950s, the long waiting times
that customers requiring repair services often must endure, the
queues for a doctor's appointment. It well may be that the
problem is more serious in sectors where supply is highly
regulated, or provided through public or not-for-profit organizations, than in sectors where there is a reasonably competitive
market on the supply side; but except in the stylized models of
some economic theorists, responsiveness to changing demand
patterns is not an automatic result of an unconstrained for-profit
supply regime.

Nor is it clear that it is impossible to devise responsive
decentralized systems without going to the unregulated market, and there may be good reasons for trying. The question of
responsiveness to changing demand conditions cannot be considered independently of the quality of response to any given
pattern of demand. While a regime of relatively unconstrained
for-profit day-care centers might have a built-in flexibility for
entry, exit, expansion, contraction, so as to follow shifts in the
market, the New York nursing-home scandals should give us
pause when we consider the quality of that response. Perhaps
because our standards are rising, perhaps because the pattern
of economic development has raised the importance of sectors
where this kind of a problem is particularly difficult, the question of how one trades off the potential static gains from regulation and other forms of nonmarket control of supply, with the
potential costs in terms of flexibility and responsiveness to
changes, is one of the more salient organizational issues of the
day. The hunt for organizational regimes that will combine
price and quality control, together with responsiveness, is
going on in many arenas, although the hunters do not always
recognize that this is what the problem is about.

Issues relating to innovation defy analysis within a static
frame. This is the reason that Schumpeter's arguments seldom

are discussed adequately within traditional textbooks. The perspective proposed above is much better suited for analysis of innovation.

Consider the questions that naturally arise when one takes an evolutionary perspective on the operation of the supply adjustment system in screening and spreading of inventions—a central issue in Schumpeter's analysis. In sectors that are organized by a "market" on the supply side, the operative "screening" criterion is profitability. In order to assess the efficacy of the market screen and spread mechanisms, one needs to study the extent to which a desirable (from some point of view) innovation gets reflected in higher profit for the firm employing it. That reflection depends on such factors as the extent to which customers are able to choose competently among supply alternatives, their willingness to switch to a supplier offering the superior product, and so on. Consumers may under- or over-value a new product. If, for example, there are important risks of which the consumer is unaware, or external effects not counted by the market or controlled by regulation, a market may not screen out what it should. Where these conditions hold there is a case for "technology assessment."

More generally, it appears much too simple minded to assert that a regime of competitive for-profit suppliers provides a good and sufficient environment for generating and selecting innovations, and that explicit governmental policies to supplement, or pre-empt, market judgments are not appropriate. In some cases, a market regime may screen innovations poorly. In others, an unsupplemented market regime may fail to generate an appropriate stream of innovations. The question of appropriate organization of R & D in our lagging economic sectors is one of the more important ones facing the nation.

But this is not the place to elaborate at any greater length on the kind of insights and perspectives that an evolutionary view of economic organization can provide. I think I have demonstrated that the framework is explicit enough to point to the structures and mechanisms that must be specified in the analysis of any sector. But the range of possible specifications of the framework is open. There is no commitment to a small set of particular stylized alternative forms. If the earlier discussion regarding the importance of quite complex forms of sectoral organization is at all on the mark, this openness and flexibility is imperative for useful analytic structure. The real intellectual commitment, the narrowing of the questions asked, is with respect to other matters. The perspective is committed to the notion that the performance of a sector is largely determined by the way in which it responds to external change, and by the way new alternatives are generated and selected.

Toward a Theory of Microeconomic Policy

A complementary commitment of my thesis is that the organizational design problem never can be solved once and for all. Organizational structures that can cope with a certain regime of technology and demand and cost conditions may not be adequate to others. This "organization obsolescence" perspective both provides a theory of policy problem genesis and maps out a role for analysis in the policy-making process.

That the analytic perspective provides a theory of how policy issues come about seems to me to be a real advantage. Some of the problems with the intellectual traditions discussed earlier stem from the fact that they contain no real theory of policy problem genesis. If we look at the full-blown logic of the policy analysis tradition, for instance, we find a flavor of solving problems once and for all. Charged with the faith that problems should be considered broadly, alternatives widely scanned, and choices evaluated in terms of a long time horizon, the policy analyst is faced with a puzzle. If, in fact, policy analysis proceeds as it should, then it would seem that sooner or later all of the problems ought to be solved and stay solved. The microeconomic theory of resource allocation (which, as noted earlier, has been closely related to the policy analysis tradition) long has contained the fiction of a once-and-for-all optimization decision at the Creation regarding everything from that day forth, and only over the last decade have theorists managed to articulate formally why this obviously ridiculous conception is, in fact, ridiculous. Clearly, no sane policy analyst ever has believed that all policy problems can be solved once and for all. However, there has been a background tone, within that tradition, that the reason why progress is so slow is that politics keeps on blocking the implementation of the wisdom of analysis. In any case, the policy analysis tradition has not contained a theory of the "policy agenda" and how the agenda changes that provides any guidance as to how to interpret and analyze a policy problem.

The "organizational obsolescence" perspective does provide a theory of the policy agenda, why it is always changing somewhat, and why it never is cleared. The commitments of this perspective regarding how a policy problem comes about, and the nature of such a problem, do provide some real clues about how to analyze the problem, and about the nature of "solutions." But this framework, like any other framework, carries the danger that it will make the analyst see things sharply that really are blurred, and perhaps even see things that really aren't there. The conception that major policy problems tend to call for organizational restructuring is inherently fuzzy around the edges. This fact should be obvious once it is recognized that "major" is a weasel word.

There is a fine line between policy issues handled *within* an organizational structure ("nonmajor" issues, from this point of view), and policy issues *about* that organizational structure ("major," from this viewpoint). A given organizational regime is expected to make decisions in a wide range of circumstances. And when that organizational structure involves government agencies in the decision-making process, some of the decisions are going to be "political"—that is, will involve "policy issues." In many economic sectors, for example, the grinding on of the organizational structure may involve budgets proposed by departments and heated debates in the legislature. The operation of regulated market sectors involves argument before regula-

tory commissions, which may hit the front page of the newspa-
pers. Antitrust proceedings (or threats of them) are common
events in many manufacturing industries. The proposition here
is that most governmental decisions are not major policy issues,
and are handled in a routine way within the system, just as most
price decisions of a corporation are routine. However, "routine
political process" does not seem adequately to characterize
what was going on about day care or the supersonic transport.
Or, to put it another way, certain significant groups of people
considered these decision problems not routine but *major*, and
therefore escalated the policy dialogue to a higher political level
than usual.

The lines between change within a regime and change of a
regime are blurred not only because politics often is involved in
routine decision making, but also because a given organizational regime contains within itself the dynamics of its own
transformation. In market structure, some firms grow, others
decline, a regime of many small competitive firms may evolve
into one of incipient monopoly, antitrust deliberations may
intervene, and so on—all without any perception that fundamental questions are being posed about the organization of the
sector. Similarly, government agencies may propose new
budgets containing new programs and new subagencies to ad-
minister these programs may be born, without the issue being
posed as to whether what is involved is a fundamental change in
structure, requiring debate in those terms.

A central argument of this essay is that often it is illuminating to view major policy debates as requiring analysis in terms
of a need to, or a proposal to, change institutional structure.
There is no scientific way I know of to test the underlying
proposition: that a given organizational regime is limited in the
range of contingencies it can handle effectively; that when
circumstances evolve outside of this range, the symptom is a
growing restiveness (on part of one group or another) with the
routine flow of events and decisions; and that successful resolution requires some kind of significant reorganization. The first

two parts of the proposition are two different ways of stating the same thing, and the last part can be considered a definition of a policy that works. The issue is, is this a useful way to interpret a policy debate?

In some cases, I suspect, clearly not. Some policy issues undoubtedly involve a particular event, contained in time or place, that can be dealt with in a compact manner representing a simple, and perhaps temporary, graft onto the flow of routine decisions and actions. To view this kind of problem as involving reorganization to deal with new contingencies would obfuscate the issue, not clarify it. If the debate about day care, or the SST, really involved just a particular investment proposal (with organizational aspects peculiar to it), then the "organizational failure" perspective would broaden the question in a way so as to confuse the discussion.

But if, as I have argued above, the particular policy issue is but one item on an agenda of issues generated by a new problem that is becoming or will become chronic, then it would seem fruitful to recognize this and stop trying to debate on a case-by-case basis. The complaints I have made about the bulk of the analyses that were done of day care and the SST are, of course, related to my proposition that the organizational problem which spanned the specific investment proposal was not recognized. The analyses contained too little history. They contained too little serious examination of the organizational structures presently involved so as to identify, and evaluate, those components whose behavior was, in effect, being complained about. And, very little attention was paid to the organizational dimensions of the proposed "solutions."

The Role of Analysis in the Policy-Making Process

The discussion above implicitly assumes that analysis can and should play a role in the policy-making process. Without exaggerating what analysis can do, I suggest that without it the

Intelligence of Democracy is not what it sometimes is cracked up to be.[5]

Over the past decade there has evolved a considerable body of economic research which takes a position on "institutional failure" similar to mine, but which (like some of the political science literature considered earlier) is far more sanguine than I am regarding the intelligence brought to the processes of institutional change. The central theoretical propositions are that when conditions change so that old institutions no longer are optimal, opportunities arise to make certain groups better off without hurting other groups; and that where there are such gains to be made, they will be made. The empirical argument used to support the theory relies on evidence that in many cases, when external conditions have changed so as to make certain old institutions inefficient, institutions have changed in plausible directions.[6]

The theory just won't wash. Even if one supplemented the theoretical propositions above with the additional proposition that all relevant parties know the alternatives and the consequences of adopting any one alternative, incentives for change by no means imply that an appropriate change will be made. In the language of the literature in question, transaction costs are high. With many players in the game, and many subgames being played, it is not all clear that all gains that can be made will be made. While the Tariff of Abominations may be an extreme case, many political "compromises" are of that sort. And evidence that something has moved in a plausible direction never should be confused with evidence that something has moved optimally. The latter requires speed and accuracy of response, not merely drift in a generally reasonable direction.

More basically, the case studies considered in this essay

[5]C. E. Lindblom, *The Intelligence of Democracy* (New York: Free Press, 1965).

[6]For a recent interesting example, see L. Davis and D. North, *Institutional Change and American Economic Growth* (Cambridge: Cambridge University Press, 1971).

indicate that, issues of conflict resolution aside, the political process does not possess sharp comprehension of the problem, the alternatives, and their consequences. Rather, the case studies show the process operating in the intellectual dark, not really recognizing what the problem is about, treating symptoms and being vague about causes, remaining unclear about alternatives as well as issues, and having little to go on in assessing the consequences of taking different actions. If the policy analysis community has often been too quick to dismiss the utility of traditional political machinery and the importance of conflict in the policy-making process, those who stress the efficiency and the efficacy of traditional machinery may greatly overestimate its intelligence, in the absence of good analysis.

I believe that analysis can play an extremely important diagnostic function. The policy issues considered earlier made their impact upon the body politic in the form of hurts and pressures, complaints and claims, that needed deeper exploration before there was any hope of other than cosmetic resolution. To say that analysis merely adds up the benefits and costs of various programs is a very misleading characterization of what analysis can do. The key role of analysis is to place the problem in an appropriate context so that one can begin to describe the nature of possible solutions.

It is conventional wisdom that the analyst can be useful in laying out the facts and empirical relations part of the policy dialogue, but that analysis should not trespass on the discussion of the appropriate weights for the relevant values and interests involved. However, in an earlier chapter I argued that it is not possible to slice clean issues of fact from issues of value. High-level values do not provide operational guides for choosing among alternatives. Low-level proximate values usually are at least as much influenced by beliefs about what will be conducive to high-level values as by those high-level values themselves. Not only is it possible to have analytic dialogue regarding proximate values, such a dialogue is necessary if knowledge is to be effectively brought to bear on the policy-making process.

Clearly the policy dialogues about the appropriate values in the day care case, and in the SST case, involved issues of fact. The sign that one attaches to the "value" of getting welfare mothers into the job market depends on one's assessments of what they could earn if they were on the job market, the relevant costs and benefits to their children of being cared for by their mothers rather than in a day-care center, and so forth. In the case of the SST, the weight one assigns to the "value" of American technological leadership per se is strongly influenced by one's belief as to the long-run determinants of comparative economic advantage.

Where analysis can lay bare the implicit factual components of value judgments, it is obvious that analysis has a role. As one pushes the dialogue about values closer to the fundamental ones, the role of analysis becomes more controversial, and the relevance of "scientific" knowledge to the policy dialogue certainly becomes more problematic. However, I would argue that even as one presses close to ultimate values, there usually is a tacit set of presumptions about facts. Analysis, if it is sensitive to the fact that important differences in relatively deep values are involved, even can be useful in the weighing and sorting out of these.

I understand full well the morass into which one ventures when one asserts that in a particular context, certain values or interests are more legitimate than others, and thus should be given greater weight. Yet I propose that the hunt for legitimate values is an important part of many policy dialogues, and that analysis can help in this hunt. It is hard to characterize exactly the elements of "fact" that are brought to bear in the sorting out of values for legitimacy regarding policy toward a given problem. Part of the matter I suspect is an assessment of saliency, in the sense that certain groups are harder his by a problem or policy than other groups. More generally, I propose that judgments about saliency derive from an assessment of Kantian consistency, viewing the particular problem as an element in a larger class, searching for a general rule for decision, within this class, that has attractive properties, and judging the particular case by this rule. In any case, I believe that as a result of the analysis of a problem it is inevitable that certain interests will appear more legitimate than others.

I hope I have been persuasive in arguing that to orient discussion of day care policy around the interests of welfare cost reduction, without considering the interests of welfare parents and, particularly, the interests of welfare children, is to neglect a key value and interest. It simply does not seem legitimate, to use the term mildly, that children's interests not play a powerful role, moderated by taxpayer interests in keeping costs down, in the governance of day care—including the determinants of the decision to attend or not to attend, and which center to attend.

In the SST case, I hope I was persuasive in positing that the interests of engineers in getting on with the building of a new airplane should not be weighted very heavily in decision making regarding final product R & D. Technological promise, as seen by engineers, might well carry legitimate weight in guiding experimental and exploratory work. But much of my analysis was concerned with arguing that consumer interests, perhaps supplemented by considerations of a broader national interest (but not as defined by technologists), were the legitimate ones in the governing of final product R & D on civil aircraft.

Political scientists have grown increasingly skittish about the concept of legitimacy.[7] Nonetheless, in normative analysis they cannot do without it. Economists long have tried to evade the concept, and as a result have been led to some rather bizarre arguments. Consider, for example, economic models of

---

[7]Perhaps the best-known attack on the concept is contained in M. Meyerson and E. Banfield, *Politics, Planners, and the Public Interest* (Chicago: Free Press, 1954).

the costs of crime. A robbery, per se, is treated as a simple "transfer" payment involving zero costs to society. The costs to society of such a crime are associated with the police, locks, and so on, in which society invests to protect itself.[8] To someone not locked into the rather peculiar arguments of modern welfare economics, this description of the "costs of crime" is clearly absurd.

I would argue that what is a legitimate interest, and what is not, usually depends on the particular context. However, I do have some general biases. The perspective on organizational structure of economic sectors that I have been developing throughout this essay views the institutions as means to meeting ends that are defined by consumers and citizens. If one accepts this perspective, arguments about the performance of the prevailing structure, and evaluations of proposed changes, should be viewed in terms of consumer and citizen interests. Put another way, producer interests per se *ought* to count for very little. A major role of analysis is to sort out consumer and producer interests, to stress the paramount legitimacy of the former, and to illuminate the policy debate in these terms.

Obviously there are some limits to this point of view; carried to its extreme, it would put analysts in the position of advocating the reduction of wage rates and profits down toward zero in circumstances where factors of production were relatively immobile and hence could be exploited by consumers without risking withdrawal of producers' services. But I doubt that this is much of a danger. Rather, the problem is the other way around: consumer-citizen interests tend to carry insufficient weight in policy dialogues in comparison with the interests of producers.

The position taken here should *not* be interpreted as in any way anti-business, anti-labor, anti-civil service. Rather, the position rests on the premise that, if applied consistently to policy questions, the primacy of consumer-citizen interests has

[8]See, for example, G. Becker, "Crime and Punishment, an Economic Approach," *Journal of Political Economy*, 1968.

a sort of Kantian quality, and that, in contrast, a syndicalist position on the issue is virtually guaranteed to make almost everyone worse off in the long run.

While economists sometimes appear to go along with the arguments above, when they get down to explicit "cost-benefit" analysis, they diverge. Thus, in the standard analyses of the cost of monopoly, the total is arrived at by netting consumers' losses and producers' gains. I am arguing that this is not the appropriate perspective from which to view, say, the growth of monopoly power in a given sector, when deliberating what kind, if any, of policy response should be made.[9] A dollar gain to producers should not be counted as equal to a dollar loss to consumers. The reason is not that on the average consumers have lower incomes than producers (which often is not the case). The reason is that policy decisions about the structure of industry should treat consumer interests as more legitimate than producer interests, and that policy makers should act to protect these.

When analysts make statements about the range of alternatives, or predictions about the consequences of choosing one or another, their discussion of the range of values involved and their saliency is grist for the political mill, not a mandate for action. Just as one would hope that the analyst's statements about alternatives and consequences involve more than hunches, I believe that the analyst's discussion of saliency and legitimacy is more than a statement of prejudices.

But I should heed my own arguments about tunnel vision and intellectual imperialism. I hope I have been persuasive that looking at institutional context and historical genesis is a much underplayed aspect of the analysis of social problems. I hope that I have at least raised some doubts in the minds of those who feel that analysis can only have something to say about how to move in Pareto superior directions, and cannot contribute to

[9]See A. Harberger, "Monopoly and Resource Allocation," *American Economic Review*, May 1954.

the deliberations about values. But I want to conclude at a more general level with some remarks about the nature and use of analysis.

In the first place, if my remarks about the role of analysis are at all on the mark, it is apparent that the fruitfulness of the analytic endeavor is determined in only a very small degree by what goes on within the narrow intellectual confines and sharp time constraints imposed by a policy analysis office. Rather, what is of most importance is the level of understanding of the underlying mechanisms and institutions, which in turn depends on the research of a far larger community of scholars —most of them outside of government—probing at the nature of social processes and social ills. The statement here should not be interpreted as advocacy of more unconstrained funds to support the social sciences. It might be more accurate to interpret the statement as an indictment. A major reason why our social problems are proving so hard to cope with is that our social sciences have been so weak. One can think of a lot of reasons. I propose that the complaints I made earlier about the parochialism of the various policy analysis camps applies with equal weight to the social sciences generally.

Over the long run I suspect that what is needed may be no less than a radical restructuring of disciplinary boundaries or, at the least, greater tolerance than academia customarily has shown to scholars with interdisciplinary interests. If I am at all accurate regarding the key intellectual problems, it is hard to see how they can be grappled with effectively unless a considerable number of able people define their interests and fields of expertise in ways that do not fit comfortably into contemporary disciplinary cubbyholes.

In the shorter run, perhaps it would help if social scientists were more honest, indeed aggressive, about saying that certain things are not well known and that those who propose solutions confidently are either charlatans or fools. Where we have strong understanding, we should say so. If understanding is strong enough, we can help develop a road map for getting to different places. But for many of our toughest problems, I suspect we do not have the knowledge to draw out reliable road maps. It is extremely important to educate the political process that certain problems are poorly understood, and that it will not be easy to find solutions that will really solve anything. At the least, such analysis can encourage a sequential experimental approach to hard problems, and can help prevent the adoption of nostrums that ultimately must disappoint and disillusion. This would be no mean accomplishment.

Index